First published 2026

Culture Matters Co-Opera ... acy—

culture foı

See www.

Layout and typesetting by Alan Morrison

ISBN 978-1-912710-70-6

Acknowledgements

Many thanks to the Books Council of Wales for financial support for this project.

Diolch yn fawr i Gyngor Llyfrau Cymru am gefnogaeth ariannol i'r prosiect hwn.

To my grandad George Cole, a conscientious objector who was willing to risk his life to save others, but refused to take another life

And

To all those who work tirelessly for justice, equity, and peace.

—Rebecca Lowe

'May God bless you with the foolishness to think you can make a difference in this world, so that you will do the things which others tell you cannot be done.'

—Franciscan blessing

Foreword

By Rowan Williams

On the morning of the day I write, more strikes on Israel from Houthi groups in Yemen are reported; Iran promises to annihilate any US ground troops who are sent to the Middle East; Lebanon protests at the killing of reporters by Israeli bombings. International concern about energy supplies continues to increase. And conservatives in the US debate whether their trust in President Trump can survive the effects of a policy directly contrary to what he and his circle have been promising for years (the answer appears to be 'Yes' for a startling number).

The endemic short-termism of contemporary politics has delivered a situation in which no-one is apparently capable of thinking beyond the next cycle of retaliation and posturing rhetoric. In a world where levels of displacement—largely caused by years of violent disruption in a range of already vulnerable countries—are unprecedented, and where the clock is ticking more and more loudly in a countdown to environmental and resource crisis, with 'extreme weather events' giving some flavour of what the next couple of decades will bring, the most powerful people in the world have chosen to pour unimaginable resources into what are quite literally unwinnable wars.

Because anyone can declare a victory and move on; but the aggressions we are witnessing are not attempts to resolve localized and specific problems. They are for the most part about the sheer display of supremacy, a supremacy defined as the power to inflict maximal damage on whole societies (civilian casualties are so far normalized that they have almost ceased to shock in terms of reporting and debate). They are aiming not at limited goals but at plain domination. And that is why no such aggression can 'win'; it will require unceasing policing, renewed displays of power, permanent fear and repression. The rhetoric is effectively about the annihilation of the other—Hamas's language about Israel, mirrored in the apocalyptic fantasies of Pete Hegseth and those like him, or Vladimir Putin's aspirations for the reabsorption of Ukraine.

And if there is no intelligible strategy for winning, there is no ceiling on the resources, national and international, human and natural, that this violence is allowed to consume.

We may be feeling nostalgic for the 'rule-based international order' that has been torn up in recent years. Understandable; but we should probably not forget that this order was itself based on a variety of deeply-shadowed moral options—not least the nuclear standoff. How often were we told that this delicately calibrated stalemate had guaranteed peace? Who can seriously make such an argument today? But more than this: that old order assumed an unchallengeable imbalance between great powers and satellites, with the latter having to carry much of the cost of the rivalry between larger states—whether in the shape of debt, inequitable trade regulations or local proxy wars. It may be preferable to the shameless moral void that increasingly prevails, and the rise of authoritarian lawlessness. But the void we see and the strongmen who now dominate so many political theatres are an index of what the old order had failed to do.

Cultures of peace

In a nutshell, the failure was in creating not just treaties and conventions but cultures: cultures of peace, co-operative interdependence, purposeful collaborative labour. In a world where the great threats to human beings—pandemic disease, environmental chaos, shrinking natural resources (as in the urgency of securing safe water supplies, just beginning to become acute on the horizon of our present conflicts)—are impossible to confine within national boundaries, it ought to be clear that building a positive culture around our shared vulnerability is the only genuinely humane future we can envisage.

And it isn't clear to so many. Today's panic, today's appeal to fearful self-protection, today's short-cut blaming of the neighbour can be made to feel simpler and safer than working out what we can jointly make ourselves responsible for. The most powerful men on earth (I do mean 'men') evidently find it much more attractive to consolidate their position by means of fostering a steady state of anxiety about strangers, within and beyond borders.

The great Australian cartoonist and essayist, Michael Leunig, whose cartoons provide a comprehensive and wonderfully resourceful course in understanding the roots of violence, says very simply in one of his books of pithy aphorisms that we are repeatedly faced with the simple choice between fear and love. As most of our religious traditions affirm, there is a real incompatibility between the two. And it is a real choice in the context of how we build a culture, nationally and internationally.

If—for example—we talk about the hope to make Wales a 'nation of peace', a major priority in the vision of the Academi Heddwch Cymru, this has to involve more than statements or gestures about MoD presence in Wales or even the involvement of local industry in arms-related concerns. These things are anything but trivial, but they are unlikely to find lasting resolution unless we are working at culture-building—and specifically building a culture and a politics in which fear is not assumed to be the final and deciding thing. Politics can't guarantee love; but it can confront and negotiate with fear. It can, by education and civic engagement, break down the despairing cynicism that makes people feel their voices are never heard; it can resource and encourage local co-operation, bridge-building initiatives that create trust. The extraordinary story of the Welsh Women's Peace Petition of 1924 which we have been celebrating in the last couple of years speaks volumes about what can be achieved by a lively, committed grass-roots culture of ethical seriousness, self-confidence, and co-operative, compassionate energy.

For such a culture-building process, we need to keep the imagination fed with language and images that push back against fear, and against the false theatre of political manipulation. As a believing Christian, I think that communities of faith have a crucial role here, if they are not to become (as, sadly, they often have been) part of the problem rather than the solution. But more broadly, the life of the arts, of poetry, music, drama and much else, is essential for the battle against fear. Art will tell us more than we might want to hear about the horrors of violence, about the appalling cost to each individual involved, from the conscripted solider to the nurse in the bombed hospital and the parent holding a slaughtered baby. Yes, in one sense it may make us afraid—but afraid not of some evil other but of the cost of our own failures to connect and understand. It will tell us about the terrible cost of violence not—as a certain kind of politician might—in order to make us angry with a convenient scapegoat, but to make us recognize how easily humans slip into the habits of mutual terror and fury, and how essential it is for us *together* to see this clearly and act for the sake of possibilities that don't just leave us in fear.

Art is an aspect of our release. The contributions to this moving, important book, which come from so many parts of the world, are aimed at stirring our conscience, our consciousness, so that we can see and act more freely. These poems and reflections are a gift to enlarge our imagining; without that enlargement, we shall lose the strength to go on resisting the fearful normalization of inhumanity that seems to surround us day after day. It is a gift to be grateful for.

Rowan Williams served as Archbishop of Canterbury from 2002 to 2012. He served as Master of Magdalene College, Cambridge between 2013 and 2020 and took up the position of Chancellor of the University of South Wales in 2014. He retired in 2020, returning to Abergavenny in his former Diocese of Monmouth. Dr. Williams is also a poet and translator of poetry. His collection *The Poems of Rowan Williams*, published by Perpetua Press, was longlisted for the Wales Book of the Year award in 2004. In 2021, he was appointed as the first Chair of Academi Heddwch Cymru, Wales National Peace Institute.

Introduction

By Rebecca Lowe

'I refuse to accept the view that mankind is so tragically bound to the starless midnight of racism and war that the bright daybreak of peace and brotherhood can never become a reality. I believe that unarmed truth and unconditional love will have the final word in reality.'

—Martin Luther King Jr, on acceptance of the Nobel Peace Prize in 1964

With conflicts and wars raging across the globe, the concept of international peace feels more elusive than ever. As I write, globally there are currently 130 active armed conflicts, the most since the end of the First World War. Conflicts are becoming more internationalised, with 92 countries now engaged in a conflict beyond their borders.

The cost, in human, economic and environmental terms, is almost beyond comprehension. Regional conflicts such as the Russia-Ukraine war and the Gaza conflict illustrate the devastating human cost and complexity of modern warfare. The Russia-Ukraine conflict has seen over 2,000 fatalities per month for almost every month in the past two years. An independent study published in the Lancet estimated that at least 75,200 people have died violently during the conflict in Gaza. In 2023 alone, conflicts cost the global economy $19.1 trillion—more than half the entire GDP of the United States—an estimated cost of $2,380 for every person on the planet.

Against a backdrop of increasing war casualties and humanitarian crisis, governments including the UK, US, France, Netherlands and Belgium are cutting back on international aid spending. In 2025, the US cut £50 billion of aid. It's predicted that as many as 14 million people could die within the next five years as a direct result of this decision. People in Gaza, Sudan, Mali, the Democratic Republic of Congo and other countries are forced to rely on this aid to survive. According to the Peace Direct charity, the UK has also cut overseas aid by almost 40%, choosing instead to divert billions into its military. But more bombs and bullets won't help us build a safer world.

So the need for international solidarity is rising, not shrinking. Research shows that peace brings prosperity, lower inflation and more jobs. Just a two per cent reduction in conflict would free up as much money as the global aid budget. 689 million people—more than nine per cent of the world's population—live on less than $1.90 a day, according to World Bank figures. Just over 10 per cent of global GDP is being spent on containing, preventing and dealing with the consequences of violence. As well as the 1.4 million violent deaths each year, conflict holds back economic development, causes instability, widens inequality and erodes human capital.

Civil strife and conflicts are driving suffering and humanitarian need to unprecedented levels. Serious violations of international humanitarian law and abuses of international human rights law continue on an alarming scale, with entire populations left without the essential supplies they desperately need. Natural disasters, exacerbated by the effects of climate change, are affecting greater numbers of women, men and children than ever before, eroding development gains and jeopardizing the stability of entire countries.

This has to change

Faced with human tragedy on such an overwhelming scale, it's easy to feel powerless. As we gaze at the newspaper headlines and their daily toll of death and destruction, it's tempting to look away, to shield ourselves from the endless cycle of violence, aggression and domination.

Perhaps, we tell ourselves, war is simply a natural part of human interaction, the inevitable consequence of living together on a crowded planet. Our cultural stories reflect this through a constant narrative of good versus evil, of 'redemptive' violence as the only proper way to resolve conflict.

But unless we challenge this narrative, nothing will ever change. And it has to change. It must. Amidst a backdrop of looming climate catastrophe, growing competition for declining natural resources and the ever-present threat of nuclear war, we urgently need to find a better way of co-existing. Failure to address this issue puts our very survival at stake. As President John F. Kennedy said: 'Peace is the most important topic on earth'.

This book contains a mixture of essays, interviews, reports, poetry and artwork around the theme of peace. Whilst many tackle the topic from a global perspective, we also honour those courageous individuals working to tackle the roots of conflict at a local, grassroots level.

As Martin Luther King Jr once said 'True peace is not merely the absence of tension; it is the creation of justice'. On a personal level, peace can mean having tough but compassionate conversations. It's not always about agreeing but having respect. Peace is equality and kindness when we are challenged. It's about being vulnerable, honest and open to criticism or difference of opinion. Most of all, it's about empathy, of walking a mile in the other person's shoes and really, honestly thinking about what life is like for them.

On a national or global level, this translates into thinking about the impact our own actions have on others, of being willing to listen, to embrace difference and contemplate change. It's placing co-operation above competition and trying to create the correct conditions economically and socially that will benefit everyone.

It is my hope that, reading this book, you will feel inspired to continue working for and promoting peace, wherever you are, and however impossible it seems. A better world is possible, and it starts here, with each one of us.

Shalom, Salam, In Peace.

Contents

1. WAR AND ITS CAUSES

Illustration: Tim Evans

Editor's Introduction

Are human beings inherently violent? It's a question that has been debated for centuries. Is aggression ingrained in our biology, or do social and environmental factors shape violent behaviour?

Anyone who has ever parented small children will know that human beings need to be taught skills such as sharing, empathy and cooperation. As a species, we are caught between two conflicting urges: the selfish instinct to survive, and the need for social acceptance. So life becomes a balance of weighing up individual and group needs.

If conflict is inevitable, war does not have to be. The vast majority of people in the world long for peace. But working for peace is not as simple as opposing wars. To create lasting peace requires working for a society where resources are more evenly and fairly distributed, creating stable governance, and more sustainable ways of living. It also requires a robust legal system,with the ability to explore restorative methods of justice, opening up paths for rehabilitation and reconciliation.

We have now reached a point in history where, for the first time, we have developed weapons so vast and numerous and so devastating, we have the capacity to wipe out the world many times over. It is therefore incumbent upon all of us to try to find better, sustainable solutions. We owe it to ourselves and to our children.

Dying Humanity

The world is too big
to talk about,
But humanity has
its essence embedded
in every life's journey.

The essence is peace,
Its manifestation is love.
When the peace walls are shaken,
The debris of humanity
obstructs the road to salvation.

Wars destroy the peace walls,
And the greatest agony:
Isn't it the cheapest
cost of human life?

We have opened our eyes
to the shrouded world,
covered with dark clouds
of destruction.

Every child can smell
the gunpowder in the air.
When a poet writes,
War is the handwriting of agony.

How uncaring would the eyes be
that do not care about the
killings of humanity?

Sushant Thapa, Nepal

The Second Horseman

Pestilence came and went.
Now War is trotting by,
His horse sprouting wings at last
so he can fly and others die.
And as for those who survive
somehow: Famine and Death
will do the rest.

The riders are keen,
but the horses are more reluctant
than they seem.

Poems Are Useless

Poems are useless
at stopping wars that have started,
But wars are more useless
at poetry than poets.
Missiles dipped in the ink of blood
write nothing worthwhile.

Rhys Hughes, Wales/Cymru

The Rubble

Is it not better
To die inside the rubble,
Than scramble out
To look around
A world you used to know?

Pat Von Bismark, UK

Song Of The Olive Tree

I am your life companion,
I bear witness to your lives,
You raised your children here,
just as you were once raised.

I see the ebb and flow of stars,
I see the changes in the air,
the rain and sun and fire,
I remain your lifetime companion.

I will always remain,
My branches and trunk remember,
Every life and death and tomb,
Every sorrow and disaster, I observe.

I give my life for your survival,
You need wood to make a fire,
To cook your bread, to eat and live,
You need to survive another day.

I am the olive tree in the courtyard,
Your house, your home, your history,
All chapters of our lives remembered,
Echoing in the land and in the stars.

Peter Devonald, UK

Peace Is Overrated

You cannot ever escape conflict, and peace is fragile; it's suspect, too. Whose peace even is it? The peace of the victor? Or state? Maybe the parent? There's no chance of a naturally occurring peace or a peace picked out by someone weaker, the loser of any conflict. Peace is whatever we say it is and that definition is often at gunpoint. Peace is always artificial with a built-in limited lifespan: the experience of company can be a provocation as much as any form of companionship.

Humanity has (while claiming to love peace) always found more ways for us to make war on ourselves, our families, our friends, our neighbours, and then all of them living further down the road and even beyond from there—everyone involved collecting resentment and waiting for release.

Maintaining that many relationships with the world, keeping the plates spinning—it's theatre and circus skills. Our brains, fine-tuned for eating berries, living inside a cave, climbing trees and hiding from things with teeth instead grapple with the microchip, the twenty-four-hour news cycle and low emission zones. And then we wonder why peace is treated as a commodity: controlled, disputed, elusive, expensive; we're ill-equipped to manage such a thing as peace for ourselves responsibly so have to fall back on processes more familiar, peace as a possession to be fought over.

Peace is never a forever peace—it's a burst for needed air after deep submersion—it's breaking the surface of the water, and it's nothing without the urgent offer of extra buoyancy and an immediate helping to the bank.

Peace can too often be a lip service response to recognised horror, legal tissue paper over a bloody wound that keeps streaming. Peace is a bully's jewel.

Peace doesn't reliably lead to justice, to restitution. Peace is the stage magician's wand, it's 'ta-da' and look away in case the illusion breaks. Yes, it is better than the warfare before, but it's insufficient. It's the worst sort of aspirational thing, and it exists in its truest form only in the afterlife. It's good only if you don't look too closely at the magic.

I scratch at my laptop keys, skin on chrome, summer sweat on my wrists, aches in my shoulders and spine, I exist hunched over the laptop, gazing everywhere I could imagine and more places I could not looking for conflict. The Romans who conquered the world at their extent knew there were other great Empires they had no contact with, nothing but pieces of foreign pottery, decorated and dusty in their hands. The Romans wanted these people and to make them kneel. And so, in the comments section I peer into and the voice channels of every single game available you can call people you've never met unspeakable names while they call you worse. One of you will win, the peace setting like the sun only when the server drops or it is bedtime.

Peace is a fairy tale told by the victor.

Martyn Sullivan, Wales/Cymru

Beyond The Gaze

Shattering is the misery of an injury
bound to libations of silence.
Mournful sum of time and space,
returns the migrant mother of the son
crucified to the disdain of crows
and torn apart between night and day
without ending nor beginning. Inhabiting
streets and houses abandoned to the memories,
in the magazines appear only photograms,
distracted words of news bulletins
in the evening on TV—just hollow noises
and frills of conscience, in dissonance.
Sweet denial follows compassion.

Ego te absolvo a peccatis tuis. *

*(Latin—Catholic formula to absolve sinners)

Lucilla Trapazzo, Switzerland

'War is capitalism with the gloves off'.

—Tom Stoppard, Czech-born British dramatist

And The Women Took To The Streets

when the barren mountain went dark,
to gather shards of fire
and remnants of life:
a leg, a humerus,
a skull cradled in their barren
wombs.
They turned them into scraps of cloth,
garments they never wore.

Silence lingered for a fraction of time
caught in the wreckage of the last bomb,
just to prove its existence.

Then, once again, the birds.

Lucilla Trapazzo, Switzerland

> *Since wars begin in the minds of people, it is in the minds of people that the defences of peace must be constructed.*
>
> —UNESCO constitution (1945)

Is Peace An Illusion?

Sometimes a pertinent question is raised;
Why, after all in this world, peace is to be praised?
When everywhere we see peace is murdered,
In broad daylight, before everyone, it's maimed.

Look at our history of great human race's intention,
It's characterised with violence, mayhem and tension.
At the same time always there the need of peace was retained,
At every interval a room for peace was maintained.

This is the game of hide and seek for peace's arrival,
This is the backup on which depends our survival.
Our very existence is for peace, bliss and contentment;
On these bases stand our society, its progress and future prospect.

Peace is real, not an illusion, not a misnomer,
Only with peace we cherish our dreams and prosper.
Cosmopolitan outlook, its expansion to every nook and corner
    of the world as such,
How difficult it may be, brings coordination, cooperation for
    lasting peace very much!

We are humans first and this is our all-time explanation,
Race, religion, region like tags are illusory justification.
Only by dint of love, tolerance, fellowship and brotherhood,
Peace like heavenly attribute can only be ensured for good.

War begets war, violence begets violence,
Peace begets peace; it's the tool of cosmic adherence.

Dr Alok Kumar Ray, India

Grieving and Despaired

1.
Grieving & despaired.
Genius & dread.
Goodness & depravity.
Glorious & dumbfounded.
A love washed away in mystery,
a gulf between bodies of history.
A wave of grief forever parting,
and souls sail from life departing //

2.
I have a tendency to burn //
bridges, letters, fingertips.
Don't touch an open flame,
certainly don't touch the same one twice.
Scars fade,
but the pattern remains.
I burn, and yearn...
for the lost,
rose tinted past,
framed stained glass
in pretty montages
forgotten history...
the lesson is less beautiful,
more bloody and pointed.

Amy B. Garratt, UK

11 September 2001

I was 14, naive, not thinking beyond playground rules or who liked who.
Walking home, chatting with a friend. I think he may have 'liked' me,
we never talked about it. Just laughs and sitting on the wall out front.

Suddenly it was 4pm, I realised my mum would be wondering where I was...
in days before smart phones. I walked through the house,
found her staring at the TV.
Watching... the day the world had changed.

The day a lot of people's changed forever.
The day a lot of people's parents wondered
if they would ever see them again.

Some never did.

Amy B. Garratt, UK

Until we can forgive, we remain locked in our pain and locked out of the possibility of experiencing healing and freedom, locked out of the possibility of being at peace.

—Archbishop Desmond Tutu

Denouement

A poem from the perspective of a dying soldier in WWI

Frailty's epitome and I, wrestling reality's grim inevitability with futility.
Fatality silently ushers me toward finality at dirt-dark Death's door.

The spectral Grim Reaper is
Phantasmagorically silhouetted afore
my flickering eyes at this damned play's
dimmed denouement.

Myriad yesterdays are described, descried
inside serial surreality for minuscule
moments.
A metaphorical curtain tumbles, eclipsing
faltering light's uncertain scintillas.

Immersed in immense opacity, transient Life
gasps its despairing last as I grasp eternal
salvation within heaven's transcendent
iridescence.

Mark Lyndon, Wales/Cymru

After Chief Rabbi's Statement 03/09/24

The following poem was written in frustration at certain Jewish leaders claiming to speak for all Jews.

You shall wake
the dream falling out your mouth
like the emergency slide of an aeroplane, screaming
before the calamity
is an event, before the event—
a decision. Don't you understand?
The problem with a nose
stud is it blends in with the ground
it claims. On hands and knees you rage
with needle and a piece of thread;
cannot get the end through what is right
in front of you. There is not time

for all the dead. Kaddish is the only Aramaic
you know, learnt from a voice-note
recorded by your dad. Even he
cannot stop a published definition
from slipping out of the wrong
palms. Soap
& pumice in the shower, you try to shed
your name. Track the water trickle
down the screen
as bombs dropping from the sky. How
even with everything extraordinary about this life
we turn to—

Gemma Barnett, UK

Whirled Peas

Like a bird's eye on barbed wire
swung in circles high and higher
holding steady, almost ready
one, two, three

Bricks to dust the droning choir
deserts gifts of Mother Gaia
no more planting just dismantling
river and sea

Missile tows in kiss goodbye
genocide by sideshow crier
general whingeing, children singeing
incensory

Safety zones slightly less dire
advertised by sky-dropped flyer
almost moving town disroofing
on TV

Heady heights which to aspire
all decked out in fine attire
crosswire sights inhuman rights
inaccuracies

To accompaniment of lyres
truth runs by with pants on fire
leaders wisely close their eyes
so they don't see

No journalist gets to enquire
banned or bombed unless complier
broken story floored and flawed
de-mock-racy

No pure race just jambalaya
destination always via
answer only minestrone
whirled peas.

Karen Gemma Brewer, Wales/Cymru

Refugee

My life is like a broken windowpane
—dreams crumbled into rain from crumbs
and memories hurt painfully.

The view outside the window
is the same and not the same.
Trunks of burned trees
stick up like exclamation marks,
the blind eyes of the houses
stare blankly ahead.

I can't hear the birds
and the chirping of the children.
The silence is interrupted
by the wail of the alarm sirens
and the terrifying
whistle of falling bombs.

How to pack the past into one suitcase?
How do I tell my child
that there is no home left?
How to shut a torn door behind me?

Alicja Maria Kuberska, Poland

Gaza

In Bethlehem
the silence becomes louder and louder
—it echoes between the sky and the earth.
The street lamps have closed their eyes,
the ruined houses are silent.
The wind blows through the deserted streets.

A crying woman can be heard in the distance.
She was about to leave
—she was left alone among the rubble
and picks through it with bloody fingers.
Hope makes her believe,
that she will hear the word "mom".

In the city,
purple dust stretches to the horizon.
The mourning sun lost its warmth and glow.
The mother found her massacred child
—and in that moment her world died.

Alicja Maria Kuberska, Poland

The Olive Branch

If the Olive Trees knew the hands that planted them,
their Oil would become Tears.

—Mahmoud Darwish

Today, as every day, somewhere
in our war-wrecked lands,
there will be funerals,
an obscene excess of them.

Some of the many mourners there
will join the war-dead soon,
being in their last hours now,
but not knowing it.
There can be no knowing.

We are all of us the same:
vulnerable under storm-clouds
of death-sentencing,
and so it has been since the curse
and grind of this war first came.

We hold hard, meantime, to the task
of keeping going, surviving somehow
against short odds, shielding our young
and our frail, cherishing our hopes,
still to be gained, still beautiful.

And yet again we bury this day
our latest dead, in grief,
and in anger, too,
born of our long pain.
So many lives lost!
So many crimes accrued!

It is not graves that should so dominate,
surely, but rather groves:

our ancestral olive groves, alive
with the meanings that they hold for us,
being givers of good, sources of wealth,
embodiers of who we are,
and signifiers of our longed-for,
long-envisaged state;

but, like each last entity that we prize,
like our very selves,
these groves are locked in a hard fight.
How long, we ask, can they—
can we?—stay strong?

Until the politics of violence abates,
these green assets will be burned,
axed, uprooted, chainsawed, bulldozed
or barricaded-off, until no crops are left:
they are soft targets
for our enemies' deep hate.

If the Olive Trees knew the hands
that planted them, a poet said,
Their Oil would become Tears.

We shed our own tears,
and with them
also our blood is shed.

Who will come to our aid?

Who will join our fight,
first to endure, and then,

when we are freed from harm,
and the likelihood of harm,
to bring in harvest upon harvest,
richly, of every type?

To you who hear our call,
including you, brave compatriots
of those who would see us killed
or cowed or dispossessed,
to you we extend the hand
of friendship
and the olive branch.

Today, as every day,
we bury our latest dead,
but never our high hopes.

We shall keep them uppermost in heart
and mind, and they will sustain us
through our future's worst, instead.

David Betteridge, Scotland

A Safe Space

What, for the common good,
can poets do, in dark times
such as these,
when love and light fall sick,
and with them hope,
and there are fewer hearts
where they can find a home?

We can keep in time and touch
with those who dream of more,
and plan for better;
We can speak with them,
and learn from them;
They are our source,
and riverbed, and stream.

We can make a safe space
for our shared thoughts,
expressing them with care,
using words that we hold dear,
keeping them warm:
thoughts and words that otherwise
might change their sense
or lose their charge.

From these we shall fashion
arguments and rally troops
that are inimical to the enemies
of justice and of peace,
for want of which the world starves.

David Betteridge, Scotland

Peace

Why there is war?
Why there is violence?
Hating and discrimination,
Why killing is there,
People are intelligent in knowledge,
But they couldn't use their knowledge,
We should celebrate unity in diversity,
We should be united,

One day we all should die,
We should love each other,
We should celebrate unity,
End war—it can't give anything,
We should love culture and traditions,
We should spread awareness,
About peace,
We should always live in peace.

Binod Dawadi, Nepal

Słowiańskie Pobudzenia

Niech zstąpi Duch Twój i odnowi
oblicze ziemi...
—Jan Paweł II

Towarzyszy mi bliskość zła
powielanie zachowań
z Euromajdanu
eksport kijowskich metod z lutego
(nie listopada-grudnia)
spotęgowany użyciem armii
czynienie ewidentnego zła
w imię dobra
po co—

nie ma rozmowy pomiędzy żywymi
jest ponad zabitymi
różna historia
mentalność język
to samo życie
czemu trzymać się uparcie
zapuszkowania
bezkompromisowości

wszechwładna oligarchia
dławi opór
eliminuje współbraci

niech zamilkną naboje
miotacze ognia czołgi
przestaną dymić opony
a przemówi rozsądek
siłą słowa poskramiaczy niedoli
złego losu na własne życzenie

na żądanie europlaców
wschodoplaców—
licha
podsycanego przez egzorcystów
zachodnich demokracji

czas na rozważne samostanowienie
na wspólny śpiewitaniec
Słowian

na Dzień Zwycięstwa

Lwów, 9 maja 2014 r

Slavic Uprousals

Let Your Spirit descend and renew
the face of the earth...
—John Paul II

I am accompanied by the proximity of evil
copying the behaviours
from Euromaidan
export of Kiev methods from February
(not November–December)
escalated by the use of the army
doing evident evil
in the name of good
what for—

there is no dialogue among the living
but above the slain.
different history.
mentality. language.
the same life.
why obstinately cling to
hard-headedness
the uncompromising attitude

omnipotent oligarchy
stifles resistance
eliminates fellow human beings

let bullets, flamethrowers,
tanks fall silent
tyres cease smoking
and reason speak
with the power of the word
of the tamers of adversity
of a bad fate at one's own request
at the request of euro squares
east squares—
a likho
fuelled by exorcists
of western democracies

it is time for judicious self-determination
for common song and dance
of the Slavs

for the Victory Day

Lviv, 9 May 2014

Slony Wiatr

Strach mnie ogarnął i drżenie,
że wszystkie się kości zatrzęsły.

—Księga Joba 4,14

Słony wiatr
rozplątuje niebu
czarne włosy

wokół księżyca
poświata z sukienek dziewcząt
komponujących mozaikę
sześćdziesięciu gwiazd Dawida

na apelu unicestwionych
niewielu ocalałych
wykrzykuje pamięć

zawstydzony Bóg pamięta

za własny grzech
nam zadaje pokutę

zapalam menorę
niegasnącym ogniem

Salty Wind

Fear and trembling seized me,
and made all my bones shake.

—The Book of Job 4:14

Salty wind
untangles the sky's
black hair

around the moon
the glow from dresses of girls
composing a mosaic
of sixty stars of David

on a roll call of the annihilated
few survivors
shout out the memory

ashamed God remembers

for his own sin
He imposes a penance on us

I light a menorah
with the undying fire

Kazimierz Burnat, Poland

(*Translated into English by Anna Maria Stępień*)

Knowledge and Mutuality

The Spanish philosopher Ortega Y Gasset offers this wisdom concerning knowledge: 'With more means at its disposal, more knowledge, more technique than ever, it turns out that the world today goes the same way as the worst of worlds that have been; it simply drifts.' This paradox illuminates the core problem of decadence within culture. A culture sans values is without objectives and hope. Ortega Y Gasset offers this concerning culture: '[...] culture is the system of vital ideas which each age possesses; better yet, it is the system of ideas by which the age lives.' Without vital ideas, the world is swamped in nihilism.

'A nihilist,' in the words of the Russian novelist Turgenev, 'is a man who does not bow down before any authority, who does not take any principle on faith, whatever reverence that principle may be enshrined in.' Since principles are taken *a priori*, they cultivate the intelligence through the emotions. Knowledge cannot exist without values. The epistemological nihilist denies knowledge exists and believes that truth is useless. In the words of American priest of the Eastern Orthodox tradition Seraphim Rose, '[...] denial or doubt of absolute truth leads (if one is consistent and honest) to the abyss of solipsism and irrationalism; the only position that involves no logical contradictions is the affirmation of an absolute truth which underlies and secures all lesser truths; and this absolute truth can be attained by no relative, human means.'

What I offer is that knowledge does and can exist through the actualization of values—Ortega Y Gasset's revelation is that knowledge is paradoxical. It not only exists, but it seemingly exists within a vacuum without sound values. He also offers this thought: 'We live at a time when man believes himself fabulously capable of creation, but he does not know what to create.' Does this apply to the current world condition? What do we create if we aspire to create through our workings of knowledge? Are there universal values to guide the student in their pursuits? We may feel thrust into a world that does not respond to our expectations, populated with disagreeable people. How we face this reality is our choice and our predicament.

A peaceful way of maintaining relations among unequal groups is shared values. In the words of Henry David Thoreau, '[...] you cannot raise money enough to hire a man who is minding his own business.' This sort of communal individualism offers the principle 'to each his own' as its standing power. People with shared values are more likely to also share respect. Johann Wolfgang von Goethe offers, 'A flippant, frivolous man may ridicule others, may controvert them, scorn them; but he who has any respect for himself seems to have renounced the right of thinking meanly of others.' To respect oneself, to know oneself, is the peacekeeper's initiation. To learn from others and develop mutuality requires self-respect most of all, and where no trace of common ground exists respect is difficult to maintain.

So what are the best methods to develop self-respect? First it is essential to recognise in yourself the divinity and dignity you represent. Each of us fills a part of the world that no one else can fill. Charles Darwin writes in *On Origin of the Species*, 'There is grandeur in this view of life, with its several powers, having been originally breathed into a few forms or into one; and that, whilst this planet has gone cycling on according to the fixed law of gravity, from so simple a beginning endless forms most beautiful and most wonderful have been, and are being, evolved.' In this context I mean to offer that no one can fill your place because you are a distinct individual. Being one of the endless forms of nature, your place cannot be filled by another. Second, one must remember to treat oneself with dignity. Take care of your health, heal when necessary, and pay close attention to your psychological wellbeing. The world needs peacekeepers and passionate people to maintain it. If you are on the route to sustaining peace and offering love to the downtrodden, you indeed must offer love to yourself.

You may be facing a tough time emotionally or physically, but bear your sufferings with dignity. Continue to add positive value to the world around you and forget the sorrows in your heart for a time. Pope Paul VI offers this piece of wisdom concerning dignity:

> Hence man's dignity demands that he act according to a knowing and free choice that is personally motivated and prompted from within, not under blind internal impulse nor by mere external pressure. Man achieves such dignity when, emancipating himself from all captivity to passion, he pursues his goal in a spontaneous choice of what is good, and procures for himself through effective and skilful action.

Control of oneself is paramount for maintaining positive relations with the world. Care for oneself and one's choices is a first step to mutuality in a world endangered by victimhood and violence. You must also learn that not everyone will agree with you or respect your ideals. However, you must maintain the art of courage. American president John F. Kennedy says of courage, 'Efforts and courage are not enough without purpose and direction.' The essence of free will is choosing a goal. How you procure your goals to achieve meaningful direction is a choice. Reflect daily about gratitude. Be grateful that we live in a spontaneous world in which everything is sustained and held together through a ground of being.

In a world of fire and torpor, it is essential to remember these principles and awake with purpose in mind. One must orient oneself to the world in some fashion. Stay inspired. Read great books and discuss them with understanding minds. Most of all, bear all things with dignity and strength, seek mutuality where there is difference, and appreciate the traditions behind you and the future you will build.

Dustin David Pickering, USA

Togetherness Defiled

I reel at the stench of the men with hate on their breath.
Those who would split us,
and spit at the brotherhood and sisterhood of humanity.
Fouling the air with their divisions and their spluttered blame,
spraying poisoned barbed words wide,
on others, always others.

Blindly they neglect the myriad of fallen who no longer breathe,
from the conflicts, wars and persecution that stole their blood.
Such mouths are cynically deaf to the hurricane of dead souls,
crying from history, begging for us to simply learn.

They dishonour all who show courage to make peace,
cruelly devaluing those with brave wisdom who care for all people,
        as people.
These traitors to love and tolerance,
have learned nothing from their wasted years on earth,
but for the malodorous scent of their own false importance.

Jim Loft, Wales/Cymru, UK

Possibilities

I've seen handcuffs, starvations, abandonments, blood, burning towers, abuses. And I've chosen to go someplace else.

Returning often to a dream, I've been seeing a world where blue is red, and the ocean is the sun, where stones stretch out towards a feverish sky in search of a little tenderness, contemptuous to gravity, screaming in elation with every tear to their toughened skin. And I've since heard and harvested that madness.

Because right here—reality—the rules are strange in all the same ways we see over there, though sensibly, the stones do not emote, and blue is in fact blue, and our ocean is little more than a well that we poison and deplete.

Up might as well be down, over here, in this waking world. Possibilities are policed, and beaten, and caged over here. Our children's shades of imagination are diminished, drained. We've been to the marches, sit-ins; seen the blunted laws and rocks thrown.

And buried behind each of our eyes, even still, even though we tire, even as we shelter, there lie outlines of a lingering liberation, away from here.

If I knew how, I would wipe the morning's saltwater from your lips and show you all the inverted colours that I see in my dreams, all that I remember of the words that rising tides failed to flood out of my mouth during the night.

You would show me your wonders too, and together we'd change this place to that someplace else, which defies gravity, remains tender when blood is spilled, nurtures, listens.

Derick Armah, England, UK

The Buck

An iPhone air raid siren clangs
The clockwork heaves the morning to
Scoop the muck from righteous eyes
The buck ends with you

Skimmed like milk to fly the planes
Lightweight payslips spit debris
Unmarked ballot papers stacked
The buck ends with me

In the morning virtue weeps
The honoured rapist shan't condemn
His loathsome lawyers' body count
The buck ends with them.

Your feed is bleeding through the screen
We're watching torture on the bus
Our MP turns the volume down
The buck ends with us.

Harvey Weedon, UK

Will Your Grandkids Smile?

Patrolling the high streets and train stations of Britain with their boxes of bloody bouquets, marching to the zealous death-rattle of the collection bucket.
Will your grandkids smile?
As you do now at noble murder,
Shed a tear and slip a quid for butchers pardoned by the imperial gag.
Will they say a prayer to George, patron saint of slaughter?
And wipe their boot heels on the memory of a hundred Bloody Sundays.
Will your grandkids smile?
When you're nose-down in the cesspool
Born in Carlisle but your corpse was found in a Baghdad suburb,
Or Helmand Province,
Or off the Kuwaiti Coast.
Bloodhounds smell deprivation
and flog laced camaraderie from disillusioned telly screens,
recruitment fund plundered from the pockets of single mothers
walking the tightrope to Christmas,
taxing NHS pay packets clutched between threadbare mittens.

Will your grandkids smile as her sickly daughter trades her shrapnel for a poppy?
And one for her son, he's just joined the cadets.
Another uniformed child smiling at bullets,
proudly dressed in fatigues not unlike yours,
the next generation of hopeful fodder,
queuing up out the door to be mangled in the war machine,
hoodwinked by politicians wearing hollow patriotism like coats.

The old lie, refuelled, must chug along,
Lest we forget, our doctrine of mournful glory,
Will your kids sell poppies? Will they shout the song?
Fresh chapters in the same despicable story.

Harvey Weedon, UK

Mohammed's Kite

"Look! It's flying!"
Mohammed with his kite
Wishes he could travel back
To the refugee camp he came from.

The kite streamers flap
Over a town of fragile tents,
Homes from scraps and scrapings.

He's found the plastic bags
The barbecue sticks
The strands of string
And teaches other children.
It's not the making he loves,
But searching up-currents like gulls.

It was blood and body parts
On their window sill
Shocked them south
Then west towards the coast.
Sounds of explosions following
Like fanatical assassins.

He makes one in the colours
Of the Palestinian flag
Raised high into the sky;
In the zone of drones
His flight of joy.

Mike Jenkins, Wales/Cymru

For Mosab

(for the poet Mosab Abu Toha)

They can kidnap the poet
But not his words.

Send them, send them out
Like pigeons from a loft,

To land on branches, splintered rooves
To visit many dusty patches for food.

Flying fast, yet not turning—
Never returning home.

Like all those who are forced
Southwards, westwards, into the waves.

But the words are their own
Villages, cities and towns—

Though their architect
Is kept trapped in bruising dark—

Look at the images, brick on brick,
Hear their rhythms' wing-beats.

Mike Jenkins, Wales/Cymru

Good Friday, 2019

(*In memory of Lyra McKee*)

Since her murder
it has been newsfeeds and tweeting and trying
to make sense of non-sense.

Here, it's as if we've been visited
by a deep Atlantic low that lours millimetres above us,
breaking barometers, suppressing articulation.

Putting its lien on the future.

But, sweetheart, the full moon is frost-framed—
a perfect scoop of lemon sorbet.
And that must do.

'Good Friday, 2019' commemorates Lyra McKee, the young journalist from Northern Ireland who was murdered in Derry in 2019.

Karen J. McDonnell, Ireland

Good Friday, 2023

'Who looks forward to having a funeral?'

—Columba McVeigh's sister, Dympna

A dead mother's rosary is there, ready to bless her disappeared boy.

The terrain is sparse, rough, biscuit-coloured. Split by a narrow road.
Cheerful machinery cuts the silence as motors come to life, though
yellow and blue police car sirens are silent. What's the rush after 45 years?
They're digging. Again.
Up at Emyvale.
Looking for that lost lad who could be a grandfather now. (Given the chance.)
He's blooming with Bragan bog as it emerges from ossifying winter:

blanket embroidered
Bog Cotton dove white
Lousewort pink
Marsh Violet purple.

Nature patterning the place before the diggers' maws desecrate it, and the gorse—
threatened with cremation—holds on to be hung on doors come May Day.

There's a mother's rosary, awaiting burial with her son—once he has been resurrected.

'Good Friday, 2023' responds to the ongoing search for the final numbers of the 'Disappeared' in Northern Ireland—specifically Columba McVeigh, who was 19 when he was abducted bythe IRA and is now missing for 50 years.

Karen J. McDonnell, Ireland

Paisley Pan

In the land of never, it never gets old.
Power sharing is an enemy pirate ship.
I was born into slingshot mouths firing
no, no, no, at the Anglo-Irish agreement.
The ticking clock buried in crocodile smiles,
refused to put down the violent hook.

The leader of the gang of boys,
saw death as an awfully big adventure,
gave up on girls who wanted family.
I blew out eight candles with a peace wish
that came true that year, when the wave
of blood wrecked my island and the boys

grew up, wanted Wendys, homes with gardens,
pensions and prison releases. Dared to grow old,
stop fighting in woods, go back to unbroken windows
in safe houses with children who grew up
on fairy stories with happy endings instead of
Radio Ulster crackling bomb warnings.

How would we remember this pan? If he'd stayed
in never never land or died at Sunningdale, ceasefire,
Good Friday or pre-Stormont? Would we think it
make believe? Paisley making peace with Natives?
Finding fairy dust and happy thoughts
to make things fly without semtex.

Imagine, today a child is born in Jerusalem
who when they're my age, might witness lost boys,
pirates, natives—laughing together, sharing power,
calling each other friend, when they die old men.
Finally acknowledging the clock
and leaving never, never land.

Cat Brogan, Northern Ireland

All human beings are born free and equal in dignity and rights. They are endowed with reason and conscience and should act towards one another in a spirit of brotherhood.

—Article 1, Universal Declaration of Human Rights

2. NON-VIOLENCE

Forgiveness is not an occasional act, it is a constant attitude.

—Martin Luther King Jr.

Editor's Introduction: Non-violence, Gandhi and Martin Luther King Jr.

Non-violence is an intensely active force when properly understood and used.

—Mahatma Gandhi

Non-violence is the principle of doing no physical harm to anybody —under any condition. It does not mean we stand idly by as passive victims of oppression. Non-violence means actively engaging in peaceful forms of resistance. For example, civil disobedience, social, political or economic interventions (e.g. sanctions, boycotts), pickets, protests, campaigning and non-violent activism.

One of the best-known examples of the use of non-violent methods to create lasting social and political change was Mahatma Gandhi's decades-long non-violent struggle for Indian independence. Gandhi understood non-violence from its Sanskrit root 'Ahimsa', literally translated as 'no injury'. Ahimsa encompasses the absence of both physical violence and passive violence—the will to injure.

Violence is rejected first and foremost because it perpetuates a cycle of hatred and vengeance. For Gandhi, violence is not the natural tendency of humans, but a learned response. Non-violence is the only true way to defeat it. Through movements such as the Salt March, Quit India Movement, and Civil Disobedience, Gandhi showed that non-violence could mobilize masses, challenge imperial powers, and achieve political goals without resorting to physical violence.

Martin Luther King Jr. was to apply Gandhi's principles of non-violent resistance during the Civil Rights movement in the United States, from 1955 until his assassination in 1968. He advanced civil rights for people of colour in the United States through the use of non-violent resistance and non-violent civil disobedience against Jim Crow laws and other forms of legalized discrimination.

In his 1967 book *Where Do We Go From Here: Chaos Or Community?* King argued: 'Occasionally in life one develops a conviction so precious and meaningful that he will stand on it till the end. This is what I have found in non-violence.' He concluded:

> Darkness cannot drive out darkness: only light can do that. Hate cannot drive out hate: only love can do that. Hate multiplies hate, violence multiplies violence, and toughness multiplies toughness in a descending spiral of destruction... The chain reaction of evil—hate begetting hate, wars producing more wars—must be broken, or we shall be plunged into the dark abyss of annihilation.

Peace is not the product of terror or fear.
Peace is not the silence of cemeteries.
Peace is not the silent result of violent repression.
Peace is the generous,
tranquil contribution of all
to the good of all.
Peace is dynamism.
Peace is generosity.
It is right and it is duty.

—Archbishop Oscar Romero

From The Land of Gandhi

Coming from India
The land of Gandhi
I believe in
The philosophy of pacifism
Where humanity rules over religion

(Om Shanti Om, I am a peaceful soul*
This sound is a sacred sound
Om Shanti Om)

I send peace and healing vibes
For war-torn nations
With a message to promote
Ahimsa and principles of non-violence
To fight against injustice and oppression

(Om Shanti Om
All sing loud throughout the
Earth and sky—Om Shanti Om)

Let us all come together
For truth, love, and compassion
Practice kindness, forgiveness
Save environment
Protect nature and its elements

(Om Shanti Om
The power of 'Om Shanti'
Can move the hardest stone
Om Shanti Om...)

**Om Shanti Om, I am a peaceful soul* is a song practiced by Bhramakumaris during meditation.

Peace Dove

It may sound strange
But it is true
Olives are not native to India
The olive saplings were imported from Palestine
And planted in a Desert of an Indian state Rajasthan
Today, I send a small branch of olive
Perhaps from the same generations old mother plant
In the beak of a peace dove
To Israel and Palestine
As a messenger of love, hope, and peace
As a symbol of harmonious time.

Poonam Chawla Sood, India

The conscientious objector is a revolutionary. On deciding to disobey the law he sacrifices his personal interests to the most important cause of working for the betterment of society.

—Albert Einstein

One Quaker and Pacifism

The following is a chapter that appeared in the book A Travelling Quaker Writes, Volume One, *published in 2019. However, the majority of it was written in June 2016 as a blog post. The audience for the original blog post was political activists, but in the book there was a wider point to be made about the nature of pacifism for a mixture of Quakers and those not familiar with Quakerism or its peace testimony.*

This essay is based on a blog that I wrote in June 2016. You might think that a lot has happened since then, but my particular prompt at the time was a mass shooting at an LGBT club in Orlando. Then, while I was writing about that, Jo Cox MP was murdered by an extremist in Britain. This was all in the atmosphere of a deeply divisive referendum campaign in the UK and the build-up to the American presidential election that was won by Donald Trump.

A couple of years later I facilitated a Quaker discussion group about pacifism and discovered that someone had not attended because he thought 'military intervention is sometimes justified'. I was very disappointed that he had not attended because we would have welcomed those views. More than that though, it is a misreading of how wide and challenging the concept of pacifism should be.

Here's what I wrote...

I have not written about the Orlando shootings as yet. In some ways I do not want to jump on a bandwagon and in some ways I am not sure that I have anything to add to what has already been written. I do think that it is relevant to me, partly because it was an attack on tolerance. Also, as journalist Owen Jones reminded people, a straight woman and her unborn child had died in the Admiral Duncan pub bombings in 1999 and those who attack 'gay venues' will kill anyone in their way. The extremist who kills indiscriminately threatens us all.

In many parts of the UK, we have a kind of tolerance to be proud of. It is by no means perfect and the rise in hate crimes is sickening, but you can still generally go to LGBTQ+ clubs and pubs in Cardiff (and indeed Aberystwyth, which had the UK's first out lesbian Mayor) without fear of anyone trying to kill everyone there.

Since the Further Education college opened on Dumballs Road in Cardiff, I have noticed young people walking there hand in hand, including same-sex couples. The events in Orlando are a reminder that the progress is good but it has a long way to go. I also noted that Owen Jones abruptly left the Sky News coverage when they tried to say that the shooting was not an attack on LGBT people specifically. The Sky News coverage suggests a deeper homophobia at work in society. I think that we cannot divorce the violent attack on LGBT people from the society that it took place in.

However, I also think that it goes even wider than that. People tend to have a misconception about pacifism, usually that it means passivity. I know a lot of very angry and very active pacifists who would disagree! Pacifism is also not just about war. That is when it gets the most publicity, but pacifism should be about the removal of all violence from society (or at least doing the most to remove as much of it as possible).

I do find it a little strange when people challenge me on it by asking what I would have done in 1914. The starting point would be not to get to the point of war in 1914. 1914 is an odd one too as it was the clash of empires, both with questionable attitudes to democracy (more adults could vote in elections in Germany in 1914 than in the UK) and both with unelected heads of state (and although the British King seemed a little less involved in politics than the German Kaiser, do recall that the King had said that he would veto any legislation that gave Ireland any kind of devolution).

Actually, 1939 is the one that people should throw at pacifists. There is no doubt which regime was the one worth fighting for in 1939 but, as I said before, the real answer would have been not to get to the point of war in 1939. The sad thing for me is that people do not connect all the violence in society and realise how it feeds off itself. Violence does not solve violence. Several years ago I was criticised on Facebook for posting the following about Libya: 'Oh good, we're going to use more violence to stop the violence. That'll work'. I would suggest that my sarcasm has been borne out by the chaos in Libya since. I invited David Cameron, Hilary Benn and Alun Cairns (my local MP) to tell me a year after the Syria vote if they felt that Syria was now more stable and less violent thanks to the violence that they supported. I wonder why they have not answered that question.

However, if we are going to avoid reaching a 1939 point again, we need to ask something about all violence in society. By this I mean the demonisation of certain groups in our society, whether they be immigrants, refugees, gay people, people with different coloured skin, 'the liberal elite', anyone who does not agree with our opinions... 'If you are not like me, then you cannot be part of my country' has become the philosophy of some. Donald Trump seized on the shootings in Orlando as proof that Muslims had to be banned from entering the USA. The shooter was, of course, a US citizen who had been born in New York and the Trump idea would not have affected him. However, it sends a powerful message of fear and hatred about outsiders.

It is more than ideas though. It is the persistence of the idea that you could hit a child if you do not like what it is doing, the lack of seriousness that is still attached to a man hitting a woman with whom he does not agree, the idea that if you are outraged by a group of people you can walk into a nightclub and shoot them, attacks that express violence and anger towards women, the idea that we only solve things in other countries by dropping large amounts of bombs on them and then walking away. All violence is connected and all part of the same continuum of rage.

A while ago I met a woman who had been married to an abusive man and who cheerily told me about how well he had been brought up by his parents, who had been sure to physically discipline him when he misbehaved. I asked her if she had ever considered that being shown from an early age that the way you deal with things that you do not like is through violence might have led to the way that he would react to her doing something that he did not like by hitting her. She had never made that connection. Why would she? We are always told that violence is random and isolated and we never look at the wider context of it.

Recently we have seen English football fans rioting in France. Who is to blame? If you read the British papers, it is the French police and the Russian fans to blame. Whereas I am not going to defend the Russian fans, what did the British fans expect when they started throwing bricks at the French police and chanting 'Victory to ISIS!'? The French are on terrorist alert and have the tear gas and batons to control any trouble. Was the policing 'heavy-handed' or should the English people have avoided being violent in the first place? Theresa May seems to be sure that it is all the fault of the French police. Phew. However, read also the reports from peaceful fans who have talked of the angry and intimidating atmosphere created by England fans singing songs about violence and beating up other nations (and the usual clichés about 'England winning' the Second World War with no mention of the sacrifices of the US, the Soviet Union, the British Empire and a whole load of non-English people). Once again, the papers support 'our brave fans' and we show that violence is okay because it is someone else's fault.

That would be a wonderfully powerful place to stop. There are politicians in the USA rushing to condemn the targeting of LGBT people in the Orlando attack who would happily deny gay people equality and who would fight for the 'traditional family' in America. I am sure that you see the point that I am trying to make about needing to stop all violence and not just warfare.

Unfortunately, today has also been a dark day in British politics with the murder of Jo Cox MP. When I saw the news of her murder, three predictions came to my mind:

i) There will be people who support Britain First and similar right-wing groups who will tweet their support for her murder. TICK, seen that, apparently she is a 'casualty of war' and therefore deserved it. Hmm ... women deserve the violence they receive ... eerily familiar from other kinds of violence against women?

ii) The suspect will be white and therefore will be excused as mentally ill (as you may know, for the media it is only brown or black-skinned people who are motivated by race or religious hatred, white people are always mentally ill). TICK, seen that.

iii) The EU Leave campaign will attack anyone who claims that the poisonous atmosphere of the referendum campaign may have contributed to the attack. TICK, some journalists have started to blog about this and have already been threatened.

It feels like a very dark day in Britain today. Yet the solution is not about a change here or a change there, it is about a wholesale commitment to remove violence from all that we do and intimidation from all that we say. That is the true pacifist cause.

Dewi Heald, Wales/Cymru

Pacifism In Microcosm

As your boot connects, I reflect
on all the ways you named me coward.
As dark blood drips from ruptured lips,
I think of how you called me weak.
As you grind my flesh to gravelled mess,
the crowd sneers at perceived fear.
As you laugh at my destruction,
I see only my reflection.

You don't see the courage spent to take the beating—
don't comprehend the strength I spend to stay my hand.
You don't dare to face your fears—control your rage—
to see yourself in me and understand.

At every wound that you inflict, my sympathy expands.
At every blow that falls, I feel who has the upper hand.
With every fading hope of glory, you're just a bit part in my story.

First published in *Song of Peace: An Anthology of Poems Celebrating International Day of Non-Violence*, ed. Prasanna Kkumar (Authors Press, 2022)

Richard Temple, Wales/Cymru

3. CONFLICT RESOLUTION AND PEACE EDUCATION

A child at Kartavya Path, India Gate, New Delhi. Photographer: Joshi Milstoner, Unsplash. Published on September 22, 2022.

Editor's Introduction: Restorative Justice

We plant seeds that will flower as results in our lives, so best to remove the weeds of anger, avarice, envy and doubt, that peace and abundance may manifest for all.

—Dorothy Day

Conflict is an inevitable part of human existence. It is how we deal with that conflict that matters. Restorative justice has an important role to play.

Traditional criminal justice is based upon a system of punishment. Those who break the law face severe penalties such as fines, probation or, in the worst cases, imprisonment. This acts as both punishment and deterrent. However, it often overlooks the needs of victims and the possibility of rehabilitation for offenders.

Restorative justice takes a different approach, viewing crime as a violation of people and relationships. It seeks to address the underlying issues that led to the crime and the needs of the victim. Restorative justice practices bring together all parties affected by a crime, including the victim, the offender, and the community, to discuss the impact of the crime and agree on steps to make amends. The goal is to reach a resolution that allows the offender to take responsibility and the victim to find closure.

In its preface to *Standards for Restorative Justice* (1999) the UN Economic and Social Council's Commission on Crime Prevention and Criminal Justice states:

> Restorative Justice seeks to balance the concerns of victim and the community with the need to reintegrate the offender into society. It seeks to assist the recovery of the victim and enable all parties with a stake in the justice process to participate fruitfully in it.

Examples of restorative justice practices include mediation between victim and offender, family group conferences, community meetings and restorative circles. These seek to repair the damage done to individuals and communities, and aim to rehabilitate the offender to prevent further crimes.

The principles of restorative justice may be used alongside the judicial system, providing alternative methods of dealing with certain crimes, especially among first-time offenders. Nationally, restorative justice was applied effectively in dealing with the aftermath of the Rwandan genocide of 1994, primarily through the Gacaca court system. At a grassroots community level, the principles of restorative justice can be used to deal with smaller-scale disputes and disagreements, and are increasingly being used in schools to teach pupils healthy ways of dealing with conflict.

> *Our work for peace must begin within the private world of each of us. To build a world without fear, we must be without fear. To build a world of justice, we must be just.*
>
> —Dag Hammarskjöld, Economist and former Secretary General of the United Nations (1905-1961)

The Peace Mantra

The year was 2007, the place was the far west of Cornwall. Seven of us, who had been meditating together for several years, decided on the spur of the moment to try something different: we decided to create a mantra. We each found a quiet corner of the garden to reflect upon what we wanted the mantra to be about.

After we returned to the circle twenty minutes later, we found that everyone had the same ideal: we all wanted the mantra to focus upon peace. Each one of us contributed something to the construction of the mantra, and by the end of the evening what we now call the Peace Mantra was born.

The Peace Mantra is simply:

Peace in my Heart
Peace in this Place
Peace in our Land
And throughout the World
Peace

The simple form of the mantra makes it easy to remember, and the words of the mantra reflected our joint belief that there can be no peace in the world without peace in our land, our community, and our own selves.

From then on, the Peace Mantra formed the basis of our weekly group meditations, and also our own individual quiet times. To begin with, we kept the Peace Mantra virtually to ourselves. After nine months a friend of a group member suggested we might consider freely offering the mantra to the wider world.

Straight away, the Peace Mantra began to form the basis of our group meditations. Each of us also used it in our daily quiet times. After a nine-month gestation period, we decided we wished to offer—freely—

the Peace Mantra to everyone in the world who wished to receive it. We decided to do this by constructing a website, by producing special Peace Mantra postcards, and by holding peace forums from time to time.

After a few years we opened a page on Facebook, which has created a good deal of interest. Both the website and the Facebook page contain suggestions not just for meditating upon the mantra, but for small practical steps each one of us can take to help build and maintain peace. Although we believe meditation is important, we believe it counts for nothing unless we base our thoughts, words and actions upon peace. This can be immensely challenging! But no matter how often we fall short, the key is to dust ourselves down, and re-focus.

We have opened a second Facebook page—The Peace Mantra in Translation—which contains the mantra translated into nearly 40 languages. Every month the Inayatiyya Healing UK (IHUK) holds an online Vigil for Healing and Peace. This is a multi-faith event, to which all are welcome, whatever their faith or none. During recent years many of the vigils have been based entirely or partially upon the Peace Mantra.

During our journey we have formed what is now called The Peace Mantra Movement to help get the ball rolling. We are completely noncommercial—how can peace ever be for sale?—and have no political or spiritual bias. (But we do engage with politicians and spiritual leaders when we consider it necessary.) Above all, we are not on a mission to gain recruits or supporters. All we care about is furthering the cause of peace.

The seven of us who co-created the Peace Mantra consist of four women and three men. Between us, our paths embrace the following traditions: Druidry, Buddhism, Zen, Taoism, Roman Catholicism, Celtic Christianity, Anglicanism, Sufism, and non-faith-specific spirituality. Right from its birth, therefore, the Peace Mantra has been essentially multi-faith. I think this is very important, as it reflects our aim to reach out gently to people of all faiths and none.

The Peace Mantra's structure is very simple, making it easy to remember. It begins with the individual (my Heart) and spreads ever further outwards, embracing the community (this Place), the environment and nation (our Land), and the entire planet (the World). This 'inside-out' approach to peace has been espoused by many spiritual leaders down the ages; the Dalai Lama and Mahatma Gandhi being two well-known examples.

However, we recognise that each person will have their own take on peace, and that they may already have found another approach, method or mantra which suits them well. We rejoice if that is so; like others, we believe there are an infinite number of paths which lead to the top of the mountain!

We encourage people to make the Peace Mantra their own. For instance, it can be added to other meditations you do. Some people may wish just to concentrate upon one or two lines; this can be helpful if they are focusing upon, say, the environment, or their own inner growth.

Some people may wish to adapt the mantra, by substituting another word for 'Peace'. For example, some people wish to focus upon Love instead, or Healing, or Light, or Joy. Some may wish to focus upon Allah, Christ, Mary, Parvati, Saraswati, Buddha—the possibilities are endless. Anything goes!

Steve Gardiner, England

The Golden Rule

The golden rule, often expressed as 'do unto others as you would have them do unto you,' is a common ethical principle found in many religions. Some examples include:

Christianity: *'Do unto others as you would have them do unto you.'* (Luke 6:31).
Judaism: *'What is hateful to you, do not do to your fellow.'* (Talmud, Shabbat 31a).
Buddhism: *'Hurt not others in ways that you yourself would find hurtful.'*
Islam: *'None of you truly believes until he wishes for his brother what he wishes for himself.'* (Hadith).
Hinduism: *'This is the sum of duty: do not do to others what would cause pain if done to you.'* (Mahabharata).
Wicca: *'An ye harm none, do what ye will.'*
Zoroastrianism: *'Do not do unto others whatever is injurious to yourself.'*

These principles foster empathy and unity across different cultures and religions.

> *Give peace a chance, yes, but why not get serious and give it a place in the curriculum: peace course in every school, every grade, ever nation. Unless we teach our children peace, someone else will teach them violence.*
>
> —Colman McCarthy, American journalist and peace activist (1938-2026)

A Vision Of Hope In Dark Days—Peace Mala

Creative education that empowers and embraces all, Uniting the world in peace

The vision and concept of the Peace Mala symbolic bracelet and educational project began in the dark days following the terrible events of 9/11—a day that changed the world forever. September the 11th, 2001 brought with it an aftermath of fear and confusion that sadly persists.

The news constantly reminds us that we are living in very troubled times. I'm sure that many of us are waking in the morning with heavy hearts. All the more reason, to do the little acts of kindness each one of us is capable of. As Mother Theresa said, 'We cannot do great things in this world. We can only do little things with great love.'

For my part, I have always tried my best; sometimes succeeding, often failing. In my 'divine madness', I have no choice but to continue to work for the Peace Mala project. Peace Mala continues to encourage children and young people to be mindful and compassionate to everyone, including the animal kingdom and the environment and our schools and youth groups really are achieving wonders!

Hope is what we must all hang on to, with faith that even in the midst of great darkness and fear, good will always prevail. His Holiness the Dalai Lama (one of the first world faith leaders to endorse the project) tells us to never give up hope! Just look at what he and his people have suffered and continue to suffer whilst the powerful nations of our world turn a blind eye. He also speaks of unconditional love as being the key to any happiness we hope to achieve in this life.

The world is mad and cruel. It has always been thus. And we are now aware immediately when disasters and horror occur. Like so many, I am often reduced to tears with the awesome cruelty some humans are capable of. However, I believe that the great challenges of living in this world give us the opportunity to grow spiritually. I'm sure you all know this too.

During the aftermath of 9/11, Islamophobia, racial and religious intolerance, prejudice and extremism rose alarmingly worldwide. Muslims and Sikhs in particular were attacked, sometimes during broad daylight. In Llanelli, the town where I taught, the Mosque suffered a racist attack and one man died from a heart attack probably brought on by the stress suffered during this shameful incident. In Swansea, the Orthodox Synagogue was desecrated. It was one of the worst attacks on a synagogue in the whole of Britain. I had also witnessed first-hand the terrible bullying of Asian and Chinese students in the school where I taught. What could one teacher do?

Approximately three months after the 9/11 terrorist attack, I suddenly thought of the Golden Rule and the Declaration of Human Rights. I realised immediately that both were a vital message for young people. But how was I to share them in a way that would be memorable? A slightly bonkers idea came to me make the learning process creative and fun! I came up with the idea of a symbolic bracelet, loaded with messages, that pupils could make in class. They could discuss the messages during the process of making the bracelet and if they liked what it stood for, they could then wear it.

The design of the bracelet and its messages took me three evenings to complete. I was aware that the rainbow is an important symbolic link between heaven and earth in many cultures. Rainbows are rare and magical and double rainbows even more so. I also realised that the rainbow design would appeal especially to children and young people.

I named the bracelet a 'Peace Mala'. The word 'mala' is Sanskrit and means 'garland of flowers'. Sanskrit is an ancient Indo-European language of India in which the Hindu scriptures and classical Indian epic poems were written and from which many northern Indian languages are derived. The 'Peace Mala' would share the Golden Rule of all faiths and also represent the human family in all its glorious diversity and Divine potential.

The bracelet comprises of fourteen coloured beads with a central iridescent clear crystal bead strung between symbolic knots. This central bead represents the wearer and the cosmos, emphasising the interconnectedness of everyone and everything. The final single bead is used as a toggle to bring the bracelet around the wearer's wrist. This represents unity, harmony and peace. Running through the Peace Mala is a simple thread which holds all the rainbow beads together. This may be called the Golden Thread of Spirituality which connects us all through the love in our hearts: acknowledging the Golden Rule and our spiritual unity opens up the pathway to peace.

With the bracelet design and messages completed it was now time to see if it would work. To my great joy it did! It spread through the school like wildfire. Members of faith communities across South Wales also welcomed it as a positive move in the right direction to encourage respect and harmony in the community.

This year we are celebrating 24 years since the official launch of Peace Mala at the UNA Wales Temple of Peace in Cardiff Wales. Our educational project has reached out across the world and has received many awards, including the praise of world faith leaders and school inspectors who have described it as a positive influence on the minds and attitudes of children and young people.

Peace Mala is about transforming the lives of children so that they become useful and important members of society. In this way they will reach out to their brothers and sisters all over the world in love and affection—the foundation for true world citizenship.

Peace Mala holds the vision of a future based on creative, compassionate education and spiritual values. Our intention is to cut through all forms of prejudice, to stand up to all forms of bullying, to support human rights, and to celebrate what makes us different from each other. Our compassionate wish is for people, animals and the natural environment to be at peace.

Pam Evans, Wales/Cymru

Those who wage war forget humanity. They do not start from the people, they do not look at the concrete lives of individuals, but place partisan interests and power above all else. They rely on the diabolical and perverse logic of weapons, which is the furthest from God's will. And they distance themselves from the ordinary people, who desire peace and who, in every conflict, are the true victims, suffering the horrors of war on their own flesh... I repeat: May weapons be silenced! God is with the peacemakers, not with those who use violence!

—Pope Francis

4. THE REFUSAL TO FIGHT

Editor's Introduction: Conscientious Objectors

"If the right to life is the first of all human rights
Being the one on which all other rights depend
The right to refuse to kill must be the second."

—Inscription on COs Memorial Stone, Wales National Garden of Peace

A conscientious objector is someone who refuses to perform military service based on deeply held moral, ethical, or religious beliefs. This refusal can stem from a variety of reasons, including opposition to war or the military-industrial complex.

In the UK, conscription was introduced during the First World War, under the Military Service Act 1916. The Act allowed for conscientious objectors to be absolutely exempted, to perform alternative civilian service, or to serve as a non-combatant in the army Non-Combatant Corps. To gain exemption, they had to convince a Military Service Tribunal of the quality of their objection. Tribunals were notoriously harsh towards conscientious objectors, reflecting widespread public opinion that they were lazy, degenerate, ungrateful 'shirkers' seeking to benefit from the sacrifices of others.

The First World War saw around 16,000 men recorded as conscientious objectors, with Quakers, traditionally pacifist, forming a large proportion. Of these, 4,500 objectors were exempted on condition of doing civilian 'work of national importance', such as farming, forestry or social service; and 7,000 were conscripted into the specially-created Non-Combatant Corps. Six thousand were refused any exemption and forced into main army regiments; if they then refused to obey orders, they were court-martialed and sent to prison.

In the Second World War, following the National Service (Armed Forces) Act 1939, there were nearly 60,000 registered Conscientious Objectors in the UK. Testing by tribunals resumed, this time by special Conscientious Objection Tribunals chaired by a judge, and the effects were much less harsh.

Conscientious objectors were allocated to Non-Combatant Corps, where roles included working in clothing and food stores, in transport, or any military project not requiring the handling of 'material of an aggressive nature'. Others worked in bomb disposal or with the Royal Army Medical Corps.

Civil work included farm work, mining, fire-fighting and the ambulance service. Almost 6,000 objectors were court martialled and imprisoned. Unlike the First World War, most sentences were relatively short, and there was no pattern of continually repeated sentences. Conscription in the United Kingdom was retained, with rights of conscientious objection, as National Service until the last call-up in 1960 and the last discharge in 1963.

Today, approximately 80 countries have some form of National Service or conscription in place. In many countries, those who refuse military service still risk years of prosecution because of their stand against war. It is more important than ever for campaigning organisations and supporters to stand alongside them.

Wounds Still Open

How many times
I have dreamed
Of that child soldier,
He oozes white blood
And not only that.

Ferite Ancora Aperte

Quante volte
Ho sognato
Quel bambino soldato
Trasuda sangue bianco
E non solo quello.

Barbara Anna Gaiardoni, Italy

There Are No Great War Poems Any More

People say the first casualty of war is truth, but they lie,
the first casualty of war is a mother and her newborn child,
caught when a bomb smashes their home and them blown
into smithereens, an evisceration, just because it could.

Dead lifeless hand, deathly pale in a fixed upwards claw,
no longer can create exquisite art or write great poetry,
no longer can touch their lover, softly, delicately,
celebrate all that is beautiful in this world.

Mud, stinking rotting mud, everywhere, festering,
as if the earth reclaims itself, one bomb and misery at a time,
a haven for rats, stink, blood and gore, sandbags and disease,
people turned to animals, trenches now, a hundred years later.

Bullets ransack bodies with indecent ease, how fragile are we?
Too dreadful to mention, too shocking, awful and obscene,
fear, terror and awareness of death at every moment,
everything we worked for crumbles, crashes down, ash.

Japanese cherry trees sprinkle mystical vivid pink hues,
strikingly magnificent confetti dreams flicker briefly
over the bodies and skulls of the living and the dead,
blood red and pink merge poetic, a terrifying tragic poetry.

Terrible scars, trauma and tragedy, is nothing sacred anymore?
We wonder what it's all for? All this violence, death and misery?
We wonder about future generations, will they seek revenge?
Be brutalised, cold to the world, live for the terrifying moment?

As leaves turn brown again, still bombs shatter lives,
repugnant red rivers flow and dreams flow with them,
away, away, reflecting all the futures sacrificed,
betrayed, denied for someone else's wealth.

Ghosts, weary and exhausted, float with deepest sorrow,
bitter shame, the wrongs and horrors linger loss, not learning,
Remember us, please, remember us, always,
and vow, never will these horrors scar again.

Peter Devonald, UK

> *We utterly deny all outward wars and strife and fightings with outward weapons, for any end, or under any pretence whatsoever; and this is our testimony to the whole world. The spirit of Christ, by which we are guided, is not changeable, so as once to command us from a thing as evil and again to move unto it; and we do certainly know, and so testify to the world, that the spirit of Christ, which leads us into all Truth, will never move us to fight and war against any man with outward weapons, neither for the kingdom of Christ, nor for the kingdoms of this world.*
>
> —Declaration of Friends to Charles II, 1660

Another World

In another world, we're laughing right now,
hugging so close, you've just found out
you're pregnant for the fourth time;
we celebrate till late into the night,
music plays, neighbours come around,
we dance and eat and drink and celebrate,
kids play till they fall asleep in our arms,
dreaming of tomorrow, dreaming of you,
another brother or another sister,
another future and another time.

In another world, we're still a family,
our children go to school and learn about
our history, they love art and embroidery,
fires of knowledge burn so bright in them,
they write beautiful poetry about love,
hope and future dreams, they believe
they can create our future, better this time,
learn from our mistakes and be brighter,
they embrace community and the world,
they shine so bright to live their best lives.

In another world, we still have a workplace,
we still have a street, we still have a home,
we still go to markets and barter and eat,
we learn in libraries and watch great theatre,
we dance and tell stories, we are the living.
In another world, we hope and plan
for our bright futures, we are like you,
we save, we dream, we eat ice cream.
In another world, we're still alive,
my babies, my loves, my love, you.

Peter Devonald, UK

900,000 Poppies: WWI Centennial In 2014

A blood-red contoured carpet flows
About the walls of an ancient dynasty
Chronicled in stone monuments.
Imprinted in each floral tribute,
A sad, distant memory, refreshed
And dug up each year for the past
Century of Remembrance Sundays.
Each rigid ceramic petal, an ossified
Blood-symbol of prodigal sacrifice;
A parched and dried-up bed of hallowed
Sanguineous petals, supported by
A raft of slender stems, each as fragile
As the thin threads of youth cut off
So cruelly, too soon. The delusions
Of 'Honour' seem neatly packaged,
A thin carapace of nostalgia for a
Sepia-tinged tribute to a 'noble' death.
But let the final word rest with that last
Man standing, Henry John Patch;
Given a 'licence to murder', called up
To shoot a man he never knew,
Against his better nature:
'Now what was the sense in that?'

Ian J. McKenzie, England

To A Tyrant

Let me look into those dead eyes
That reveal no hint of emotion—
A total disconnect between the lies
Spilling from your mouth, the promotion
Of an opportunist propaganda
Machine, churning out a well-worn story,
Justifying the means, while you gerrymander
The truth as cover for the gory
Consequences of your ego's lust;
To top the pinnacle of history's
List of shameful dreams of conquest,
In your attempt to resurrect past glories.

Let the fate of others be a lesson to you—
As Caesar fell, so in time, you will too!

Ian J. McKenzie, England

The Principle of Peace (After Thomas Ellison's Scrapbook)

11:33 pm and I'm trying to pull poetry from pixels,
place people at the nib of a pen I'm chewing
and speak breath into bodies so I can better tell their tale.
I'm laptop-lit as fingers click through a jaw slackening
book of scrap (in name), but it's numbing by nature
to wrangle recollection written in real time by a man
whose morals threatened the might of the machine.

Be it enacted by the King's most Excellent Majesty...

...words from the travesty of conscription laid out in law, the
proletarian precursor to shock and awe as Mother Empire
made up her face and readied for a last hoorah.

12:27 am and the counterbalance of confusion
is keeping my rage at bay as I tip-toe upstairs, scared
to consider that *my* treasure tips the scales on the wrong
side of truth. What proof lies dormant in darkness?
Breath-held and blind I fumble in the bedside drawer
and scoop pewter in the palm of my hand. This watch carries
whispers from a foreign land and gleams from 1915 with the
gallantry of my Gran's Great Uncle George who when wounded
won a medal for saving a man worth so much more than he.
And to this day, we have kept his name alive. And I know
that's right, but I wonder tonight if he really *had* to die?

(As an aside, 4 months later on the day he died he was
1 of 9,000 killed on a single sodden field...)

1:44 am and they're *still* refusing to rip flesh from bone
but their words alone shake shackles as they see comrades
clattered to the call of COWARD! How craven to hunker
in the face of hanging by way of hard labour, and all for their paltry

principle of peace. There was no conditioned release contained
within The Manifesto of the Absolutists, and yet their
parched throats sung and the Red Flag rung through bars to rise above
bomb blast to a battlefield that saw combatants bedecked
in robes. Decision makers in denial as they tapped-time to a dance
in which death begot death whilst packaged as pact and the
threads of untruths were woven as fact, and the years,
they yowl to the cry of 'what for?', but the reply, in their own words
reads War creates War.

Scott Cassidy, Scotland

Brothers and sisters of every language, people and nation: we are one family that weeps, hopes and rises again. No more war, a journey with no return; no more war, a vicious cycle of grief and violence.

—Pope Leo XIV, Prayer Vigil for Peace, April 2026

Conchies—A Pacifist Farming Community

An architect, an insurance broker, a journalist, a painter and decorator, an artist, a bespoke shirt-cutter—these are just a few of the unlikely people who came together to create a farming community in the Lincolnshire villages of Legsby and Holton cum Beckering during World War Two.

At that time, RAF Wickenby in Lincoln was a hub of military activity from where hundreds of bombing missions were launched. One thousand and eighty of the young men involved in those missions were killed. Just a few miles away, however, the neighbouring village of Holton cum Beckering, became a hotbed for the Peace Movement. A group of like-minded people gathered together in this farming community, united in one belief—they were not going to fight World War II.

The community was one of a number of pacifist farming communities that grew up around the country during the Second World War. Although farming duties were largely taken over by land girls, replacing the farmers sent away to war, it was also something a conscientious objector could do. The farming cooperative which formed in Legsby and Holton cum Beckering attracted conscientious objectors—or conchies, as they were known locally—from all over the country.

The Lincolnshire pacifist community grew out of a chance meeting at the Peace Pledge Union between Roy Broadbent, an architecture student whose father owned a large engineering firm in Huddersfield, and Dick Cornwallis, an Oxford graduate and accountant whose father was British ambassador to Iraq. Both were conscientious objectors, both had been disowned by their fathers. They wanted to do something practical, so they set up the Community Land Training Association, to give pacifists who believed they had a vocation for community farming an opportunity of being trained under an experienced farmer. Local farmer John Brocklesby agreed to lease them one of his rundown farms, Collow Abbey Farm, and provided basic training. New trainees, most in their late teens and early twenties, started arriving on bikes, as young men, and a few women, from different parts of the country and different backgrounds, left their city lives to farm rather than fight.

The community had a lasting impact on the areas and many of them and their descendants went on to achieve remarkable success. A co-founder of the group was Roy Broadbent. He was the father of Oscar-winning actor Jim Broadbent whose acting debut as one of the children in Ibsen's *A Doll's House* took place in an old prisoner of war Nissen hut where the community put on plays. Another key member was Francis Cammaerts who worked as a shepherd before leaving the community to become one of the most celebrated figures in the French resistance movement. His nephew Michael Morpurgo wrote the famous *War Horse*. A slightly later arrival at Halton was the architect Edmund Albarn, grandfather of Blur frontman Damon Albarn.

Community member Donald Sutherland left his job in insurance, aged 22, to join the community. He was influenced by Aldous Huxley's *Ends and Means* from which he concluded 'Whatever the aim you have, aim to use the right means to achieve it. You don't achieve peace by making war.'

The work was hard. He recalled lifting sugar beet by hand ('I was a pussy man, not used to that sort of thing'). 'It was a difficult thing, taking a stand, when you know other people have suffered,' he said. 'But it was really a community feeling. We all got the same amount of money and we had family allowances before the government brought in family allowances. The experience completely saved my life.'

The story of the conscientious objectors who set up Pacifist Farm Communities in Legsby and Holton cum Beckering during World War 2 was brought dramatically to life in 'Remembrance', an original documentary play by Ian Sharp, written specially for the Broadbent Theatre. In the play, the conscientious objectors (the 'conchies' as the local people called them then) tell their stories mainly in their own words from the interviews many of them later gave. ‘Our aim is simply to tell the truth, as far as that is ever possible, of this remarkable phenomenon at a remarkable time,’ says writer Ian Sharp, ‘but hopefully in a lively, entertaining and thought-provoking way.’

Ian Sharp, England, UK

Non-violence confronts systemic injustice with active love and refuses to retaliate with further violence in any circumstances. In order to halt the vicious cycles of violence, it requires a willing acceptance of suffering and death rather than inflicting suffering or death on anyone else.

—John Dear, American peace activist, author and former Catholic Jesuit priest

Remembrance Day

"Hi Dad. How are you?"
"I'm fine" he replies
from 1939.

Horse earth
furrowed under heavy feathered feet,
hooves moving slowly over fenland peat
in the warm, war-time morning.
Steam breathes from the heat of her skin.
Her name is 'Pink'.

My father follows unadventurous,
careful, quiet, conscientious,
lines ploughed straight,
filled with guilt
at distant killing
in which he will not participate.

He turns over the confusion of principles
as he labours the flat land.
The black soil conceals a mingling
of pride and shame; he struggles to understand.

Every day
Pink plays clever.
Seeking to evade the tightness
of harness
she distends her velvet belly,
holds her breath: "Yes,
This time!"
But he knows the trick,
waits for the inevitable exhale.
She gasps out stale air

and quick deft fingers
grip, fasten straps,
trapping Pink.
The game is up!

At dawn
the siren warning.
A firebomb, unexploded,
has landed outside on the concrete lawn.
Yawning awake he stares from the corner
of his small, worn window.

At 19 he is 'Designated Fire Officer'.
Braced with bewildered responsibility
he prepares for some unpredictable inevitability.
But a consternation of 'Air Raid Precaution Wardens'
(torches flashing, self-important talking)
is already considering a course of action.

Their low voices play counterpoint to the wail of the claxon.
Eventually, a clatter of metal bucket, a scraping of spade on stone,
two men shovel up the problem, carry it away, their shapes
receding into the grey unknown,
casually chatting with nonchalant innocence, defensive
indifference.
He interrupts his story, chuckles into the phone
at these primitive methods of bomb disposal,
wondering why it did not detonate
and recalling relief at his missed moment of glory.

Late one afternoon they found a dead zebra by a roadside bend—
incongruous, wondrous in the English fenland,
left behind by a travelling circus.
In absence of a better plan the farm workers
sawed her into quarters

and dropped the dismembered carcase
down a well.
No-one considered what befell
those who drank its exotic waters.

War ended in celebration and song.
Pink, legs broken, long gone,
firebomb inert, forgotten,
zebra still contaminating and rotten.

He turned his back on the god of his parents,
his childhood of non-conformist compliance
and sought forgiveness from science,
volunteering for medical experiments.
Telling no-one he waited for plague or pain
or a death that never came.
Year after year of pointless self-blame.

So,surprised at his survival,
still alive at 95,
his voice is growing slow.
"I don't know
how I got so old" he says.
"My legs are rather cold,
I'd better go".

(My father was a conscientious objector during WW2 and worked as an agricultural labourer, looking after German POWs. This is his story as told to me one afternoon during a very long phone conversation. It is all true—yes, even the zebra!)

Rosy Wood-Bevan, Wales/Cymru

Grandma Stepped Out With A Conchie

Grandma stepped out with a conchie,
and it gave her family such pain.
Cousins, uncles, the callow boys
she'd been raised with—all signed up to fight
without complaint. Her parents knew
too well what war would cost, that some

would come back maimed, some would be lost,
yet nothing could match the shame she'd bring
to them, the wounding of their name.
An attack on all her father felt
was right. None could explain how his daughter
could fall for a coward, lose her heart,

her self-control, ignore her sense
of duty. How normal, how much better,
had she been sweet on a youth
in uniform. But no. His girl
threw herself away on a traitor.

Girls and women would pursue them,
as they strolled arm-in-arm. Then came
white feathers. They called him lily-livered,
and her a disgrace, spat in their faces.
He went to be a stretcher bearer,
put himself in harm's way, of course unarmed.
Came back frail, terminal; expired
in a sanatorium.
Lucky escape, her family said.

Grandma mourned her fallen conchie.
He'd always be 'the one'.
She wasn't brave, just tired.

Grandad knew he was second choice,
second best, cannon fodder like the rest,
but he survived four years of war. He'd get
the prize, win his bride, start a new life...
with the girl who'd walked out with a conchie.

Simone Mansell-Broome, Wales/Cymru

Peace is not an absence of war, it is a virtue, a state of mind, a disposition for benevolence, confidence, justice.

—Baruch Spinoza (1632-1677), rationalist Dutch philosopher.

5. DISARMAMENT

Editor's Introduction: Steps Towards A World Without Nuclear Weapons

Over 12,000 nuclear weapons threaten our survival today, even though the majority of people in the world and their governments support an international ban on their development and use. Nuclear rhetoric around the wars in Ukraine and Gaza has shown us how these weapons can make a dangerous situation ever riskier. The possibility of a nuclear war is the greatest for many decades.

But there is another way. In 2021, an historic United Nations treaty banning nuclear weapons became international law. The United Nations Treaty on the Prohibition of Nuclear Weapons makes it illegal under international law for its signatories to develop, test, produce, manufacture, acquire, possess, stockpile, transfer, use or threaten to use nuclear weapons. It also makes it illegal to assist or encourage anyone to engage in these activities. So far, 95 countries have signed the Treaty and 75 have ratified it. The Campaign for Nuclear Disarmament (CND) is lobbying the British government to sign and ratify the treaty and work towards the global elimination of nuclear weapons.

The requirement for nuclear disarmament has also been enshrined in international law since 1970, in the form of the nuclear Non-Proliferation Treaty (NPT). The NPT commits its signatories—including the UK—to take steps to disarm if they have nuclear weapons and not to acquire them if they don't.

While the non-nuclear states have kept their side of the bargain, all the nuclear powers still have their weapons and are even upgrading or modernising their arsenals. There is still a long way to go before we can contemplate a world free of nuclear weapons. However, the UN Treaty on the Prohibition of Nuclear Weapons represents an important milestone. The Treaty is a breakthrough in international disarmament efforts and will be of enormous support in achieving the goal that most of the world shares: that there is no place for these weapons of mass destruction.

Love Your Nuclear Bomb

We have learned to love the bomb.
It is not clean, but it is not wrong.
It keeps the peace. That's a fact.
So please don't you overreact
When we shall sing with joy
For Fatman and Little Boy.
The bells will ring a thunder knell
Like a door closing in the depths of hell.
Big Ben shall be like that frozen clock
When protesters cry and poets mock.
The organ then shall sound a siren call
That will echo around every wall
For fleets of missiles and Trident subs
In the hope they will be no duds.
Smite our enemies with fire and ash
For Nuclear Bombs we got the cash.
And if the Earth burns like a second Sun
Remember not what we lost, but was won?

(*On the 3rd of 2019 there was a Thanksgiving Service for Britain's nuclear deterrent in Westminster Abbey, London; the Campaign for Nuclear Disarmament held a protest outside. The poem was on the* Poetry 24 *website.*)

Phil Knight, Wales/Cymru

Non-Disposable World

Picture IT—a world without THERMONUCLEAR OVERKILL
Bomb lost its thrill,
It Will It Will
Picture It—a world after all the BOMBS are GONE
TOO FAR MON
Bomb lost its thrill,
It Will It Will

PICTURE IT a world not holding its breath
at the edge of death
the toxic waste the chemical taste of food in MONEY ONLY GOOD.
Bomb lost its thrill,
It Will It Will

PICTURE IT!
no mad generals with pointing digit poised
EARS PINNED filled with NOISE of SHOUTS OF DOUBTS
Bomb lost its thrill,
It Will It Will

PICTURE IT! a world after the end of Biological Weapons
which fools will send threaten.
Bomb lost its thrill,
It Will It Will

PICTURE IT!—no fanatic dramatic climactic climate war
no inversions or floods or earthquakes conned crunch
too much heat then or dry no clouds in the sky no rain with lunch.
Bomb lost its thrill,
It Will It Will

PICTURE IT no ray guns in space
no thistley whistley missiles, to bless the stratosphere torn

or HOT HEADS WIND DOWN, BURN after space war
rafter thought it'd meant quite a lot.
Bomb lost its thrill,
It Will It Will

PICTURE IT the bombs gone
the missiles dis-missiled
the sub de-commissioned no reactors out fission
PICTURE IT the control board turned off
did I hear a scoff?
Bomb lost its thrill,
It Will It Will

Always Another Anti-War Poem

Seems as I lay
my placard down
Then some other, goll damn, other-guess crown.

Has found some banner, or cut one down
And wrapt it up in wonder thunder, or flung it down

On the bloody, muddy spattered ground.
He rankled and waved, cause we're stocking the graves
With sons and brothers, and many innocent others from us and
some other mothers.

Sons who smiled, and waved at flies
Instead of break bashing basking bloody bread-boulders by.

Richard W. Spisak, USA

World Court Project—New Zealand

New Zealand has been a nuclear-free zone since 1984, when Prime Minister David Lange banned nuclear-powered and nuclear-armed ships from using New Zealand ports or entering New Zealand waters.

Under the New Zealand Nuclear Free Zone, Disarmament, and Arms Control Act 1987, territorial sea, land and airspace of New Zealand became nuclear-free zones. This has since remained a part of New Zealand's foreign policy.

New Zealand's four-decade anti-nuclear campaign is one of the few successful movements of its type in the world which resulted in the nation's nuclear-weapon-free zone status being enshrined in legislation. But campaigners weren't content to stop there. They wanted to challenge the legality of nuclear weapons on the world stage.

The World Court Project was started in New Zealand in 1986 by a retired Christchurch district court judge, Harold Evans, and initially led by New Zealanders. This civil society campaign aimed to have the International Court of Justice (the highest legal branch of the United Nations, also known as the World Court) give an advisory opinion on the legal status of nuclear weapons.

Over 32,000 New Zealanders signed 'Declarations of Public Conscience' condemning nuclear weapons and supporting the World Court Project in the early 1990s. Worldwide, they collected nearly four million signatures—an enormous figure in the age before online mass-petitions.

After years of campaigning, the Project had its international launch at the UN in Geneva in1992. The three core co-sponsoring organisations were the International Peace Bureau, International Physicians for the Prevention of Nuclear War, and International Association of Lawyers against Nuclear Arms.

In response to persistent, strategically applied pressure and lobbying by World Court Project members, the UN General Assembly adopted a resolution in December 1994, asking the Court urgently to give its opinion on the question:

Is the threat or use of nuclear weapons in any circumstance permitted under international law?

New Zealand Policy

New Zealand was the only Western-aligned country to vote in favour of the General Assembly resolution calling for a World Court advisory opinion on the legal status of nuclear weapons. In the resulting Court hearings, New Zealand firmly stated that nuclear weapons reduce international security, and that the threat or use of nuclear weapons should not be permitted under international law:

"In New Zealand's view, the sooner [the threat or use of nuclear weapons are banned], through the progressive development of international law, including the negotiating process, the more secure the international community will be."

(New Zealand Statement to the World Court, 1995)

World Court Project members worked to ensure as many countries as possible made strong arguments in favour of the illegality of nuclear weapons. This included:

- advising many of the governmental legal teams;
- delivering almost four million 'Declarations of Public Conscience' to the Court from individual citizens around the world asserting the inhumane, illegal nature of nuclear weapons; and
- successfully advocating, for the first time ever, for the Court to hear evidence from 'citizen witnesses' who had personally suffered the effects of nuclear weapons.

Many other countries made similar statements to New Zealand, arguing that nuclear weapons are illegal under international law. Australian Foreign Minister Gareth Evans, for example, declared that the use, threat of use, acquisition, development, testing and possession of nuclear weapons are illegal, since 'nuclear weapons are by their nature illegal under customary international law.'

The outcome

On 8 July 1996, the International Court of Justice delivered its historic Advisory Opinion, entitled 'Legality of the Threat or Use of Nuclear Weapons.' The Court, by majority, ruled that:

'The threat or use of nuclear weapons would generally be contrary to the rules of international law applicable in armed conflict, and in particular the principles and rules of humanitarian law'

and agreed unanimously that:

'There exists an obligation to pursue in good faith and bring to a conclusion negotiations leading to nuclear disarmament in all its aspects under strict and effective international control.'

Ever since 1996, the New Zealand government has linked this important ruling to its more progressive disarmament objectives, advocating strongly for the elimination of nuclear weapons.

Further information on the World Court Project, can be found at www.disarmsecure.org.

Kate Dewes, New Zealand

Word and Deed

He,
who has the gift of seeing
a possible evil future
—acts.
He gives his voice to the reason of the people of the world,
and knows,
that the atomic bomb brings death.

He,
who takes the Hippocratic oath
—heals,
but also knows
that for individuals and nations the most important
is not only health, but also peace.

He,
who is able to cement
the wisdom of words with deeds
does not need to take oaths
to prevent the collapse of reality.

Eliza Segiet, Poland

Translated by Dorota Stępińska

6. RADICAL FORGIVENESS

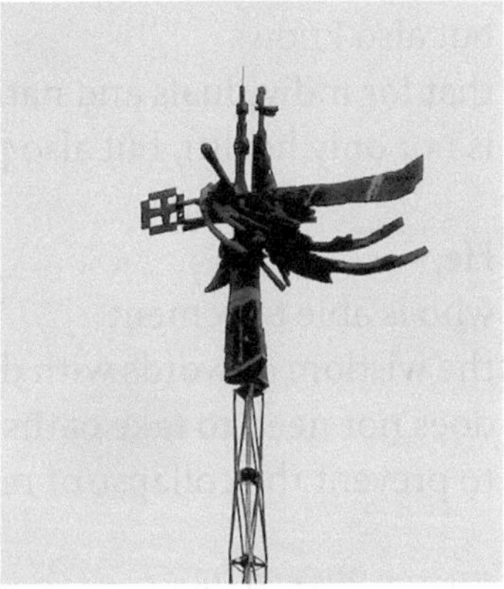

Editor's Introduction: Forgiveness

Forgiveness is a conscious decision to let go of resentment and anger towards someone who has harmed you. It does not mean forgetting or excusing the harm done, nor does it necessarily require reconciliation with the offender. To quote Corrie Ten Boom: '*To forgive is to set a prisoner free and discover that the prisoner was you.*'

A concept of forgiveness is found in most religions. It is central to the Christian concept of grace—that we are to forgive others, because we have ourselves been forgiven. In Islam, Muslims believe that Allah is merciful and forgiving, and they are encouraged to forgive others as a reflection of their submission to God. The Qur'an states that those who forgive will be rewarded by Allah (Qur'an 24:22). In Judaism, the concept of Teshuva (repentance) involves acknowledging wrongdoings and making amends, highlighting the communal and relational aspects of forgiveness. In Buddhism, forgiveness is viewed as a way to release attachment to anger and resentment, which aligns with the path to enlightenment.

Forgiveness is not the same as forgetting. It does not condone, excuse or pardon. We can condemn someone's actions and acknowledge the harm caused, yet choose to remove ourselves from any desire for revenge or retribution.

In many contexts, forgiveness is granted without any expectation of restorative justice, and may be granted without any response on the part of the offender. In practical terms, though, it's easier to forgive someone who shows accountability for their actions.

Forgiveness does not necessarily mean reconciling with the person who caused harm. There may be valid reasons for choosing not to reconcile —safety, trust or personal boundaries, for example. Reconciliation is an additional step, not a requirement.

Forgiveness is a deeply personal choice, and ultimately an act that only the wronged person can choose. Expecting or pressuring someone to forgive can cause further harm and risks re-victimising them and adding layers of guilt. Sometimes, forgiveness feels impossible, and it's okay to admit that. However, for those able to move towards an attitude of forgiveness, it can open the path to self-healing.

> *While I was Canon for Reconciliation at Coventry Cathedral, I presented these crosses in places like Bujumbura in Burundi...To this day that cross remains within the sound of gunfire. This symbol is not one of ivory tower isolation: it speaks into the very heart of the wars, torture and terror that so fill our world.*
>
> —Archbishop Justin Welby, 2016.

Coventry's Cross Of Nails

Healing wounds, living with difference, building justice and peace

'As a global leader in Christian reconciliation, we show that journeys of transformation from darkness to light aren't just possible. They happen here, every day.'

—Dean John Whitcombe, Coventry Cathedral

'We are trying to banish all thoughts of revenge. We are going to try to make a kinder, more Christlike world.'

—from Provost Howard's 1940 broadcast, made from the ruins of Coventry Cathedral on Christmas Day, six weeks after the Blitz

Coventry was the only English cathedral to be destroyed in the Second World War. On the night of November 14, 1940, the city sustained heavy bombing from the German Luftwaffe, intended to destroy Coventry's industrial infrastructure and munitions factories.

At 7.20pm the first bombs fell, not long after the air raid siren was sounded. At 8pm, Coventry Cathedral was hit and flames soon engulfed the building. Over the course of the night, the Luftwaffe dropped 500 tons of explosives, 30,000 incendiaries and 50 land mines. More than 43,000 homes were destroyed and 554 people killed, with a further 864 severely injured.

In a single night, the cathedral which, for centuries, had stood at the spiritual heart of the city was reduced to a pile of smouldering ash and rubble. The day after the destruction of the Old Cathedral, Provost Dick Howard (who led the cathedral during WWII) made a commitment not to seek revenge, but to strive for forgiveness and, ultimately, reconciliation with those responsible. At the time, this was seen to be very radical thinking, as Britain was still at war with Germany.

After the Blitz, two symbols emerged from the rubble: two charred roof beams, which had fallen in the shape of a cross were bound and placed at the site of the former altar, and three medieval roof nails were also formed into a cross, which became the original Cross of Nails. This is now located at the High Altar in the new cathedral.

Shortly after the Blitz, the words 'Father Forgive' were inscribed on the wall of the ruined chancel. A Litany of Reconciliation is held at midday daily during the week, which pays homage to this inscription, written in 1958 by Canon Joseph Poole.

The destruction of the cathedral touched the hearts of many countries around the world, who contributed and gifted elements of the building of the new cathedral. The decision to leave the ruins as they were after the Blitz became a powerful symbol of peacebuilding and forgiving enemies.

The Cross of Nails quickly became a potent symbol of friendship and hope in the post-war years. In September 1947 a Cross of Nails was presented to St Nickolai Church, Kiel, Germany, a symbol of peace between former enemies.

In the following decades, several hundred crosses of nails have been given to various organisations, including churches, prisons and schools. The new cathedral, rebuilt next to the ruins of the old, has become a centre for peace-making and reconciliation around the world. The partnerships that emerged from the war became the international Community of the Cross of Nails, which continues to grow globally to this day.

Coventry Cathedral is living testament to the truth that death and destruction do not need to have the final word. Forgiveness and reconciliation is not just possible, but the only true way to end the cycle of revenge and violence.

Rebecca Lowe

People's Prayers Saved My Life—Tearfund

Tearfund is a Christian charity that partners with churches in more than 50 of the world's poorest countries. The charity and its partners tackle poverty through sustainable development, responding to disasters, and challenging injustice. This is a Q&A with Jeff Woodke from Tearfund partner, Jemed, who was held hostage in West Africa for more than six years. (A version of this article previously appeared in Tear Times *magazine).*

Interview with Jeff Woodke by Peter Shaw

Jeff Woodke, a US humanitarian worker, was taken captive by terrorists in October 2016 and released in March 2023. Jeff is the former head of Jemed (Youth WithA Mission) a Tearfund partner based Abalak, northern Niger. At the time of his abduction, he had stepped down as head of Jemed and returned to monitor the organisation's work.

Jeff was abducted by gunmen who shot and killed his guards and was taken to northern Mali. Over more than six years of captivity, he was beaten, locked in chains for hours a day and endured self-imposed hunger strikes. The US government negotiated his release alongside Olivier Dubois, a French journalist. His wife, Els, campaigned tirelessly for his release, for many years not knowing he was alive.

At Jemed, Jeff pioneered 'sustainable nomadism', a process that enables nomadic pastoralists (livestock farmers), their families and animals, to withstand drought while retaining their traditional way of life.

We are very grateful for Jeff agreeing to talk so candidly about his time in captivity, his faith and life back home...

How are you Jeff, how are you doing in yourself?

I'm working on getting better. There's physical issues, there's emotional, there's psychological, there's spiritual issues. Everything has its own pace, rhythm and time.

How have you changed as a result of your experiences?
There are changes in every dimension of my life. The person I was when I was taken into captivity was not the person that came out. I kept my faith. Actually, my faith kept me. That's probably the best way to say it. The big challenge we've been facing, my family and I, is how to get healed from post-traumatic stress disorder, from all the physical things that I have from my captivity. And how to redefine being human, my situation and what it means. So that's the road we're on.

Have the experiences you had changed the way you think about Niger and the people you were there to serve?
Yes and no. I was held, for most of the time by the Tuareg people in the mountains. It was very difficult for me to be treated the way I was treated by them and by the Fulani people. These are people for whom, for 30 years in Niger, I had poured out my life. It's been very difficult for me to come to grips with the people that took me. But forgiveness is something I practised while I was a hostage. At every opportunity I got, I would forgive my jailers. Because I knew that if I didn't do that, I would break completely. I was already broken by the end. Forgiveness is just something you have to do day by day.

How did you manage to get through each day. Did your faith help?
I would pray fast for two or three days. My captors would get angry at me if I fasted because I would get sick. But I felt prayer and fasting was the way out. When I could walk, I would walk, five or six kilometres a day. I would worship and pray, and then I would go back to whatever little shade that I had and I would pray. I had a routine.

But after a year, two years, three years, of fasting and praying... man. It's like prayer isn't working for me. My body started to deteriorate. My leg was already bad. I just couldn't walk. Hope went real soon. Hope that I was ever going to go home was completely gone by my fifth year. As my hope went out the window, my faith began to drop and my time in prayer ended.

In the end, I just couldn't do much anymore. I was hunger-striking. I had terrible malaria that just about killed me. I was physically, and emotionally exhausted. I didn't even want to come home. I just wanted to be over. But I couldn't let go of my faith 100 per cent. I just couldn't. I would try and then it would just come back into me: 'Got to pray.' I would pray for my family out of love, and I would continue to try not to be angry at God out of love. And that was it. That was it.

How has your faith been since you came back?
When I recovered, I quickly found out that there were people all over the world who had been praying for me. I found stacks of letters and cards and things. There are children who have been praying for me since they could speak. People all over the world prayed for me. In my own prayers, I prayed for a lot of specific things. When I came out, I saw my prayers had been answered. I had no way of knowing. But I saw that these prayers had worked. Things just fell together through prayer.

People's prayers are one of the things that saved my life. And that's my message to everyone who prayed for me or even sent thoughts. Your thoughts and your prayers. They work. Through prayer, God literally raised someone from the dead. Because I was done. I was a walking cadaver. That's all I was. But I'm home now. Thank God.

What are your feelings towards the people who took you captive now?
I want to walk free, so I can't hate. And if I feel that anger, I have to learn to let it go through me and out of me. And not to be carried away by it. You have to forgive, you have to love, you have to accept. It's up to people to make their peace with God. You're going to catch a whole lot more flies with honey than with vinegar. That's it.

Please continue to pray for Jeff, Els and his children as they continue to recover together and for Jeff's physical and mental health.

Peter Shaw, UK

Forgiving

From the sinews and neurons, half-healed tendons, that
remind me of you, I call across this chasm
of caution,

if love is persistence, perhaps this bruise is love instead?

A friend said, *let the picture be shredded and thrown.*
So, I hurl that night's image a hundred times—let it
fall
and fall again, glazed eyes shining back
the punch of a secret,

and it returns—adrenalised—the wall thuds, quaking glass, your
hand's grip, furl of lip,
claws to my jaw, frozen limbs, crashed against my door, your words on
how

I'll
never amount to more.

Now
I'm washed in the angry rain from valley mountains,
so high they know the gasps
of each sunrise, that revenge
is nothing, but forgiveness is

the long poem,
long reason,
is the *Ho'oponopono*,
is holding a candle over tarot,
taking to the sea on Sundays,
is sweating into the swing of a punch bag,

is watching you leave, rageous, gruff looks,
mumbling through the vodka, one last quivering slap, all hearts close
to collapsing.

I've tasted this unimaginable air,
been misted with shame,
and now, in the space of forgiving—soul's finest act of creation,
I unlock my door, see
your shadow leave,
the lightening of your thunder,
over a new line,
unfurling into
white sun—

the rock of your punch, undone.

Guinevere Clark, Wales/Cymru

7. ACTIVISM AND PROTEST

The Peace Petition from the women of Wales to the women of America. (From left to right: Gladys Thomas; Mary Elizabeth Ellis; Annie Jane Hughes Griffiths; Elined Prys.) The Welsh Women's Peace Petition was signed by 390,296 women.

(Photographer: Harris & Ewing, public domain image Wikimedia Commons).

Editor's Introduction: Two Peace Movements

'Dripping water hollows out stone, not through force but through persistence.'

—Ovid

'May we hand down to the generations who come after us, the proud heritage of a Warless World'

—Welsh Women's Peace Appeal to America, 1923.

Peace is not only a noble vision for humanity; it's a call to action. Individually, it's easy to feel powerless against the relentless tide of wars and conflicts across the globe. But collectively, the power of our voices and our actions is far greater than we might imagine.

In 1923, in the aftermath of the horrors of the First World War, the women's committee of the Welsh League of Nations Union (WLNU) organised an unprecedented appeal. Said to be seven miles in length, the Women's Peace Petition was signed by 390,000 women appealing to the women of America 'from home to home' and 'hearth to hearth' to join them in a call for Law Not War: for the United States to join and lead the new League of Nations.

The Women's Peace Petition was a truly remarkable Wales-wide effort, involving almost every household, through peace activists going door-to-door collecting signatures. A delegation led by WLNU chair Annie Hughes Griffiths travelled from Wales to America in March 1924 for a two-month peace tour of the States, building support through American women's organisations involving over 60 million people. In 2023, following a campaign supported by the Wales Peace Academy/ Academi Heddwch Cymru, researchers and activists, the Welsh Women's Peace petition returned to Wales, where it is now lodged in the National Library of Wales.

Another internationally-recognised peace movement with Welsh roots was the Greenham Common Peace Camp. On August 26th 1981 a group of 36 people, mainly women, started their 100 mile walk from Cardiff to RAF Greenham Common. The group, calling themselves Women for Life on Earth, were protesting against the American government holding cruise missiles on common land. They soon realised that a march alone was not going to be enough to get the missiles removed and began setting up camps around the edges of the base. The first blockade of the base occurred in March 1982, with 250 women protecting and 34 arrests.

In September 1981, 36 women chained themselves to the base fence. On 29 September 1982, the women were evicted by Newbury District Council but set up a new camp nearby within days. Their campaign sparked national attention and in December 1982, 30,000 women joined hands around the nine-mile perimeter fence at the Embrace the Base event, in response to the third anniversary of NATO's decision to house nuclear missiles on British soil.

On 1 April 1983, about 70,000 protesters formed a 14-mile (23km human chain from Greenham to Aldermaston and the ordnance factory at Burghfield. Another encircling of the base occurred in December 1983, with 50,000 women attending. Sections of the fence were cut and there were hundreds of arrests.

The last missiles left the base in 1991 as a result of the Intermediate-Range Nuclear Forces Treaty. The camp was finally brought to a close in September 2000 after 19 years of protest, with the old camp being inaugurated as a Commemorative and Historic Site on 5 October 2002.

Though nuclear weapons are no longer housed at Greenham Common, activism against their stockpiling and potential deployment continues with ongoing protests at bases such as Faslane and Aldermaston.

A Lifetime of Peace Activism

Alison Lochhead interviewed by Rebecca Lowe

The date was March 17, 1968. A bright-eyed teenager set out from Swansea on her first peace demonstration—one of an estimated 10,000 people marching in London against American action in Vietnam and Britain's support for the United States.

Alison Lochhead, then aged 16, had told her parents she was visiting the capital to stay with a friend. She hadn't mentioned the peace march, fearing it might worry them. What she encountered was a real eye-opener. "It was quite brutal. The Police started kettling the crowd. We managed to escape up a side road, but others were penned in; it was really frightening. But it didn't put me off attending other marches. If anything, it hardened my resolve."

This was to prove the start of a lifetime of peace activism and campaigning. "I was brought up in a family concerned by social justice; my grandfather was against the WW1 and my parents against WW2, and I joined CND as a teenager," says Alison.

In 1981, the Greenham Common Women's Peace Camp was established to protest against nuclear weapons being placed at RAF Greenham Common in Berkshire, England. At the beginning Alison was working abroad but visited when she could and took part in actions and other actions associated with Greenham Common. "We had a brilliant telephone network. You'd receive a call and phone ten people and they'd phone ten more and in no time at all, you'd have amassed thousands of campaigners, hence getting 40,000 to surround the base."

In 1984 she moved from Bath to Wiltshire and joined the Bradford-on-Avon Peace Group, which was active in Cruise Watch. She recalls nights following the Cruise missiles when they left Greenham Common: "We were in our Morris 1000s and clapped-out vehicles. Hilarious. The MoD police could be brutal. They'd blockade us and drag us out of our cars. We had our tyres slashed. Our phones were tapped."

Alison was part of the 'Snowball' actions which saw women surrounding other military bases in the UK, with the intention of being arrested. She connected with other Greenham Women on the 40th Anniversary march to Greenham in 2021, and they have since campaigned as Greenham Women at Faslane, COP26. They were instrumental with many in starting Lakenheath Alliance for Peace, campaigning to stop the US bringing nuclear weapons back to USAF Lakenheath, Suffolk. Unfortunately the US did bring back nuclear bases to USAF Lakenheath in 2025, so the protests and camps are now to get rid of them.

A more recent concern is deep-space surveillance satellites planned in Pembrokeshire and the use of Wales for the Military and AUKUS (Australia, UK and USA alliance) and the use of military drones. "Currently drones are programmed but have a human being behind them, directing them," says Alison. "However, the military is working on, and now uses, autonomous lethal weapons—programmable drones and other weapons that can be used to target people with no human contact at all. We are living in frightening times."

Now in her seventies, Alison, who is an artist and member of the Royal Society of Sculptors, shows no signs of easing up on her peace activism. "There's so much going on that people don't even hear about—weapons being tested and transported across the country," says Alison. "The way various parts of our political world decide to colonise others and continue to asset strip for resources—currently the horrendous news of Palestine, Ukraine, Sudan, plus endless others. Demonstrations and awareness-raising need to keep happening. It is hard to keep up with what the UK government and USA and others are doing to curtail free speech and statements against genocide; and their continuous involvement with making the world a very frightening and unsafe place in 2026."

"A lot of the time it can feel like nothing changes, but gets worse, but I'll never give up working for peace. We have to let people know what's going on and provide an alternative voice to all the militarism which is all around us. If we didn't, things would be even worse. So we can't afford to stop. We have to keep going."

Alison Lochhead, Wales /Cymru

We should think carefully about the reality of war. Most of us have been conditioned to regard military combat as exciting and glamorous—an opportunity for men to prove their competence and courage. Since armies are legal, we feel that war is acceptable; in general, nobody feels that war is criminal or that accepting it is criminal attitude. In fact, we have been brainwashed. War is neither glamorous nor attractive. It is monstrous. Its very nature is one of tragedy and suffering.

—The Dalai Lama

Greenham In Light

Looking for my sister all day in light
With photos meshed across the fence.
A jacquard Argyll of memories crunching among gravel
Flowers in sunny speckled mushroomed woodland
Multicoloured knitted lines of interlocking women in a 'do si do' of willow stripping
From nose to nose with sentries looking at us trying to be serious
You are supposed to be serious
'I am very serious—these are my babies on the fence'
I pin my babies to the links as a cheerful swarm of women sway in light
She's here somewhere
Not finding her won't matter because the day itself has been significant
Her woolly hat will be as bright and battered as the next one
She makes up the numbers after all
But seeing her will be a proof
The day darkens and a trudge emerges as our buses are released from custody at air force camps
Air dampens us the mothers of the missing fathers, husbands, sons and lovers
I may go home to Wales without the proof of her
But with an eventide fast falling on tens of thousands of us and an abiding memory of the tunes
To songs which are not really very good but they are of course very very good
Draining away with exhilarated feet to join the motorway umbilical
We swing across the gravel
A woman beats the window of her accelerating bus
Wild eyes and my mother's wave
My sister there's the proof of love

Heather Pudner, Wales/Cymru

Diary of A Peace Activist In Palestine

(Written in November 2023)

'I couldn't contain my empathy, my anger, or my amazement.'

I have spent most of my adult life engaged in solidarity and justice work with and for Palestine, and alongside the small yet vital Israeli peace movement. I have mostly lived and travelled around the West Bank, but the last time I saw Gaza, I was standing beside the border with hundreds of Israeli and international peace activists protesting a heavy Israeli bombardment of that small place and the people in it.

I don't have the words to even begin to understand how it must feel to be a Palestinian in this moment, when your very humanness is so starkly being brought into question; when so many of the most powerful governments in the world are supporting a massacre of your people, and we are all witnessing genocide in real time.

And neither do I have the words to begin to understand how it must feel for so many people in global Jewish communities to witness the largest mass-killing of Jewish people since the Holocaust. There is a rise in antisemitism, and there is a rise in Islamophobia and anti-Arab racism all over the world.

And all of the people experiencing this are just human beings with soft hearts, like us. People who sing lullabies to their children, who dream of becoming scientists and artists, medics and carers. People who argue with their families and who fall in love, drink coffee and eat too many sweets.

I first visited Palestine in my early 20s. I spent two weeks travelling all around the West Bank, not long after the end of the second intifada, in a mixed international group of about 20 young people being hosted by Sabeel, the liberation theology organisation based in Jerusalem.

I met so many different people and learnt so much. I was completely taken aback by the injustice of the whole situation. I couldn't contain my empathy, my anger, or my amazement at the resilience, creativity and love shown by the people I met on that trip.

One of the experiences that imprinted most deeply on me was watching a young Palestinian man being stopped at a checkpoint in Al Khalil (Hebron) and being arbitrarily humiliated (being made to pull his trousers down) and beaten by Israeli soldiers. I, and others, were (rightly) shocked by this event, that I have since come to learn is just a 'normal' part of everyday life for so many Palestinians living there.

And then the settlers arrived. In Al Khalil there is a particularly extreme community of right-wing (armed) Jewish settlers. They harass the indigenous population on a daily basis; they have driven hundreds of Palestinians from their homes and forced the closure of the main shopping street to Palestinians.

Some of our group were Palestinian citizens of Israel. The settlers, with machine guns slung over their shoulders, started trying to harass and separate these members from the rest of us. We instinctively tightened the circle around our friends who were more at risk, but still the situation escalated until the settlers managed to get the Israeli soldier at the nearby checkpoint to arrest one of our group—the same soldier we had just witnessed humiliating and beating a local resident.

Very soon, a member of the international Christian Peacemaker Teams (CPT) arrived and proceeded to try and secure the release of our friend who had been arrested.

After a fairly drawn-out saga, she was ultimately successful and we all headed back through the checkpoint together, under ongoing intimidation from the armed settlers.

This was the moment I knew I would go back to Palestine and that volunteering as an international observer would be the thing I could offer. However unjust it is that the Palestinian population need people from distant countries to bear witness, to help to safeguard their right to live in their homes while being treated with basic human rights, while that is the reality, at least that was something I could offer.

I thought I would write this diary piece about how full of grief and despair, how incandescent with rage, how dazed and overwhelmed I have found navigating the past month and all of the complexity, the simplicity and the loss of it all.

But I find myself instead reflecting on how utterly amazing it is that for all these years the Palestinian people I have met—in Palestine, in Israel and all around the world—hold themselves with such *sumoud* (*steadfastness*), dignity and patience; that the foundational resistance of so many Palestinians is simply to keep trying to grow and harvest olive trees, to keep living in their homes, despite all of the structural and physical violence they experience, and to keep living with as much joy as they can share with their family and friends.

And I also find myself reflecting on the size and entrenchment of the ongoing occupation of Palestine and all that goes with it. The reality is that the current escalation of violence in Palestine (in Gaza and in the West Bank) and Israel didn't start on 7 October 2023. It is a continuation of a much longer conflict, and the systemised oppression of the Palestinian people by the state of Israel, whether in Gaza, the West Bank or in Israel, is ultimately the thing that has to change for real justice and real peace to be achieved.

Penny Stone, Scotland

Sandals

The shoes are worn
uncomfortable
with sharp points
on the inside soles
mine are not much better
I try on yours
and you mine
then repeat
so there's no blind spots
when you walk, you feel how it is
and when I plod along I feel the same
each step another bit of suffering
another bit of shame
we try them on again
and repeat
until we are high up
on the hill,
you can see for miles and miles
from up here.

Declan Geraghty, Ireland

8. CULTURAL ACTIVISM

Guernica in Lagunillas, Málaga, Spain. Mural by Miguel Ángel Chamorro, 2015. A mural reproduction of the painting Guernica *(1937) by Pablo Picasso. Photo by Daniel Capilla. (Wikimedia Creative Commons).*

Banksy mural in Bethlehem 25 July 2015. (Photographer: ZaBanker, Wikimedia Images CC).

Food Not Bombs *mural, Berlin. Founded in the early 1980s in Cambridge, Massachusetts, Food Not Bombs is a global volunteer movement that shares free vegan and vegetarian meals to protest war, poverty, and social injustice. (Photographer: Hogre. Source: Creative Commons Wikimedia Images).*

Editor's Introduction: Art as Activism

'Great protests are great art works'

—Diego Rivera

All art is revolutionary. In a world which commodifies everything according to monetary worth, creating something of intrinsic value feels like an act of rebellion.

Art can be a powerful catalyst for political and social change. Throughout history, artists, musicians, writers and dancers have used their creativity as a powerful social commentary. As Bertolt Brecht famously said: 'Art is not a mirror to be held up to reality, but a hammer with which to shape it.'

A powerful example is Picasso's *Guernica*. Painted in response to the Nazi bombing of the town of Guernica during the Spanish Civil War, the painting sparked international condemnation of the bombing. First displayed at the 1937 Paris World's Fair, *Guernica* not only called attention to the horrors of fascism but also became a universal symbol of peace, referenced in countless demonstrations and peace initiatives ever since.

In our own times, Banksy's *Love is in the Air*—also known as *Flower Thrower*—has been embraced as a powerful symbol of peaceful resistance after it first appeared on the West Bank Wall in Palestine. Banksy's image depicts a masked protestor throwing a bouquet of flowers as if it were a grenade or Molotov cocktail—recalling the protests against the Vietnam War in the late 1960s, where activists presented flowers to armed police. This, in turn, took inspiration from the Beat poet Allen Ginsberg who, in his November 1965 essay titled 'How to Make a March/Spectacle,' proposed that protesters should be provided with 'masses of flowers' to hand out to policemen, the press, politicians and spectators. Artistic activism can challenge authority. Subvertising is a form of art which uses the traditional iconography of advertisers to make a political point. At the 2015 Paris COP21 climate conference, the collective known as Brandalism installed 600 posters that attacked what they perceived as the hypocrisy of corporate sponsors. In 2022, billboards in London, Bristol, Manchester, Sheffield, Brighton, and 11 other European cities, were hijacked to highlight the role of airline emissions in the climate crisis.

Arts at the grassroots level can break through social apathy and political impotence, giving a voice to those who have been silenced by systemic injustice, and providing a platform for protest and advocacy. To quote Spanish-Mexican filmmaker, Luis Bunuel, 'A writer or painter cannot change the world. But they can keep an essential margin of non-conformity alive. Thanks to them, the powerful can never affirm that everyone agrees with their acts.'

The very act of creating promotes healing and hope. To create is an act of empathy. It invites others to see the world as we see it—encouraging empowerment and engaging dialogue, across cultural and social divides. Art can also, as we have so often seen in recent times, provide a powerful outlet of expression for those caught up in conflict. Out of the ashes, we rise up dancing, reclaiming ourselves for what we are—powerfully human.

Under(Found) Poems by Kevin Searle

The following are two concrete/visual poems that are simultaneously pieces of street art. The first pays homage to anti-racist activist and former American football player, Colin Kaepernick, and the second, Marxist, feminist activist and philosopher, Angela Davis. They are part of a broader series in which visual artist Kevin Searle has tried to re-imagine London Tube roundels as progressive political figures with striking natural afro hairstyles.

Colin: A Blackout Poem

(The pre-Nike deal version)

Kevin Searle, England

Angela: An Under(found) Poem

Kevin Searle, England

Imagine Peace Tower

Power works in mysterious ways. We don't have to do much. Visualize the domino effect and just start thinking PEACE. Thoughts are infectious. Send it out. The message will circulate faster than you think. It's Time for Action. The Action is PEACE. Think PEACE, Act PEACE, Spread PEACE PEACE is POWER!

—Yoko Ono.

The Imagine Peace Tower is a striking light installation on Viðey Island, near Reykjavík, Iceland. Conceived by Yoko Ono as a tribute to her late husband, John Lennon, it serves as a global beacon for peace and hope.

A powerful beam of blue-white light is projected vertically into the sky, often reaching altitudes of up to 4,000 metres (13,000 feet). True to Iceland's environmental focus, the tower is powered entirely by geothermal energy.

The Tower consists of 15 searchlights with prisms that act as mirrors, reflecting the column of light vertically into the sky from a 10 metre-wide wishing well. Buried beneath the monument are over one million written wishes collected by Ono through her global 'Wish Tree' project. The tower is not lit year-round. It shines from 9th October (Lennon's birthday) through 31st December, ending in the new year.

Visitors can view the tower from the Reykjavík shoreline or take a short ferry ride to Viðey Island to see it up close.

To submit your own wish to be included in the memorial's archives
email wish@imaginepeacetower.com or send a postcard to
IMAGINE PEACE TOWER, PO Box 1009, 121 Reykjavik, Iceland
www.imaginepeacetower.com

Rebecca Lowe, Wales/Cymru

Radical Music—Too Big For Words (July 2024)

'All you need are three chords and the truth'

Radical music is so often about the core message. We think so carefully about the words we choose to communicate something we feel is important.

We find musically wrapped words that help us as a community of humans to process many painful injustices in the world around us. But there is a bigger thing that music, and singing together in particular, can bring us and that is somewhere we can hold and experience emotions that are simply too big for words.

Even as a campaigner and songwriter, if I think about the realities facing so many millions of my human cousins, I struggle to find words to express the pain, the sadness and despair of so much of what is happening to people all over the world simply because of inequality and greed. And, equally, I struggle to find words to express the size of feelings of hope and joy experienced throughout the natural world and global human family.

Despite this, as writers and songwriters, we of course try to find the words! But there is always something more, and for me that's where I find music. For other friends of mine, it is through dance or the visual arts that they process this 'beyond verbal' world and make connections but for me, and so many others, it always comes back to music.

Throughout the 20th century, enslaved people forcibly transported from across the African continent to the United States kept singing to express the pain and injustice of their lives. They used these songs not only to build community with each other, but to build resistance, even singing songs to communicate to each other hidden route maps for those attempting escape. These songs kept thousands of people's spirits alive through the most unthinkable experiences, and helped thousands escape, literally saving many more lives.

Since the 1970s, lovers of punk music have gathered together, often in dark, dank and sweaty rooms, pogoing up and down, sing-shouting along with a band proving that all you really need are three chords, as long as you sing your truth. Though it was radical folksinger Woody Guthrie who coined the phrase 'all you need are three chords and the truth', punk carried it forward with pizzazz.

Punk continues to open up doors for people to imagine possibilities that would otherwise feel locked. Imagining social systems that work differently is inherently part of it, but so is the experience of making music and dancing together as equals, regardless of anything. If you can do it, so can I, and if I can do it, so can you. But with more swearing.

The singing revolution that bubbled across Estonia, Latvia and Lithuania in the late 1980s brought together thousands of people to sing in defiance of the Soviet occupation of their home countries. This massive scale of protest and 'national pride' singing ultimately helped emancipate all three of these countries with less bloodshed than we have seen in so many comparable conflicts in the world. And they still regularly gather together in their thousands to sing these same songs, expressing and defending their freedom with their collective voice.

In the early 21st century, a small but dedicated underground heavy metal movement flourished in Baghdad. Some musicians ultimately left Iraq and pursued their music elsewhere, but others remained in their country, expressing their powerlessness around both the internal politics of their country and region and the US invasion of their home. The dense musical soundscape of heavy metal music is the perfect soundtrack to express the realities of war, amplifying the truth written in the words. Truths such as '(we) grieve for what turns to ashes and bones and buried beneath the garden of stones' and 'They start the war and we pay the dues, no we won't fight any longer'. But it is the driving guitar, bass and drums so central to heavy metal music that give such emotional catharsis and strength to the lyrics.

Singing in the streets at our weekly Gaza vigil these past few months, we have seen so many people walk towards the balm of music expressing something inexpressible. People stop to listen and to sing with us, and to shed tears that hold both pain and relief. We are connected with each other as we sing together, and we are connected to those who hear us and take time to listen. And for all of us, the music is sometimes a comforting balm and sometimes a furious roar, expressing something beyond our collective comprehension.

But we are together, and together we feel something.

Penny Stone, Scotland

> *Any form of art is a form of power: it has impact—it can affect change. It can not only move us, but make us move.*
>
> —Ossie Davis, actor, director, writer and activist

The View Of Others From A Different Perspective

A Poetry-Art Installation by Antje Stehn and Geneviève Seydoux

Inaugurated 5 September 2024, Das Kleine Kunsthaus, Bern, Switzerland

In an era fraught with turmoil, the ever-present headlines of war, violence, and suffering often feel overwhelming. With diplomacy faltering and the international community struggling to prevent unimaginable atrocities, the question arises: How can peace ever be restored? A transformative shift in perspective is vital—a shift that fosters empathy, the power to understand the thoughts, intentions, and motives of others. The exhibition 'The View of Others from a Different Perspective', created by artists Antje Stehn and Geneviève Seydoux, offers a space where such a change in perspective can begin.

Held at Das Kleine Kunsthaus in Bern, Switzerland, this installation is a powerful exploration of empathy, violence, war, and hope. Through their collaboration, Stehn and Seydoux invite viewers to engage not only with the art but with the voices of poets from across the globe, presenting a diverse and heartfelt response to the themes of conflict and peace. The exhibition space was designed to evoke a sense of unity amidst chaos. Antje Stehn's hammock, delicately filled with dandelions, hung across the room, symbolizing fragility, peace, and the potential for new beginnings. Surrounding the hammock were Geneviève Seydoux's stone sculptures, which took the form of body parts—fragments that suggested both the brokenness caused by violence and the enduring resilience of the human spirit.

The installation was complemented by twenty-four poems written by international poets from a diverse array of countries. These poems, translated into German, were a crucial part of the installation, reinforcing the central message of the exhibition: the importance of understanding and connecting with others across cultural and linguistic barriers.

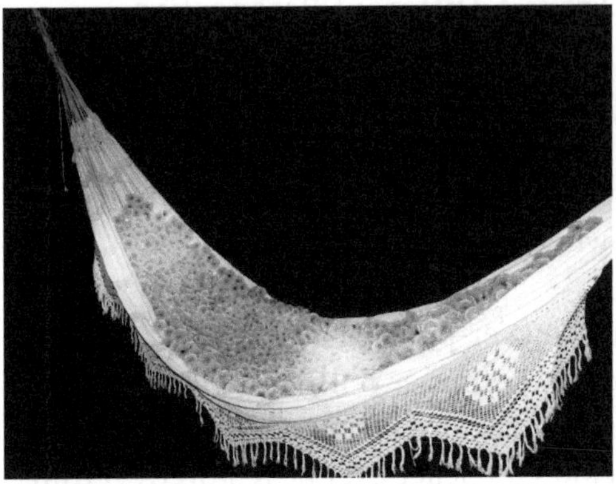

https://youtube/wo544Bl2ulc
Youtube link to the video

With the participation of:
George Wallace, USA
Genevieve Zongolo, Süd Afrika
Đặng Thân, Vietnam
Lucilla Trapazzo, Schweiz
Gili Haimovich, Israel
Angelo Gaccione, Italien
Nahid Ensafpour, Iran-Deutschland
Tamer Öncül, Zypern
K Srilata, Indiien
C.C. Arshagra, USA
Sabrina De Canio, Italien
Ekaterina Grigorova, Bulgerien
Gino Leineweber, Deutschland
Laura Cantelmo, Italien
Jawdat George Eid, Palestina-Israel
Pankhuri Sinha, Indien
Giancarlo Sammito, Italien
Reha Yünlüel, Türkei
Salem Khafani, Iran-Deutschland
Betty Gilmore, USA
Arthur Zimmerman, Schweiz
Simona Albano, Italien
Antje Stehn, Deutschland
Andrea Grieder, Schweiz

A video screen displayed the poets reading their works in their mother tongues, creating a rich tapestry of sound that included Arabic, Hebrew, Persian, Vietnamese, Turkish, Spanish, and various Indian languages. This multilingual experience recalled the biblical story of the Tower of Babel, where the unity of humanity was divided by language. However, in the context of this project, the blend of languages did not create division but rather underscored the shared human experience—the collective yearning for peace.

The poets, who partly hailed from countries directly impacted by conflict and war, brought their personal perspectives to the exhibit. Each poem was a window into a unique experience, yet collectively, they painted a picture of a world united in its need for peace and understanding. The diversity of languages and voices was a reminder that despite our differences, art, poetry, and the desire for peace transcend all barriers.

Empathy—an ability not just to feel, but to understand—is essential for bridging the divides that separate us. Empathy is not only a moral imperative but also a source of strength and hope.

Antje Stehn, Germany

The Red Dress Project

The Red Dress project by British artist Kirstie Macleod is a global collaborative embroidery initiative that has provided a creative platform for marginalised individuals, primarily women, to share their personal stories of identity, resilience, and empowerment through needlework.

Made of over 87 pieces of burgundy silk duplon, the dress incorporates work and embroidery styles of 380 people from 51 countries, making it a truly global multicultural creation.

Created over 14 years, the Red Dress Project is a powerful statement of peace, solidarity and beauty which transcends borders, cultures and continents. The Red Dress began as an exploration of identity, transforming into a symbol of unity and voice. Amidst global challenges, its message of collaboration and compassion resonates stronger than ever, inspiring hope for a more connected and empathetic world.

In a world which feels too often fractured, where the voices of intolerance seem to grow increasingly loud, the Red Dress Project is a remarkable example of what can be achieved when we celebrate our diversity and work together to create something beautiful.

Rebecca Lowe, Wales/Cymru

Novi Sad Protest—Occupying Public Space

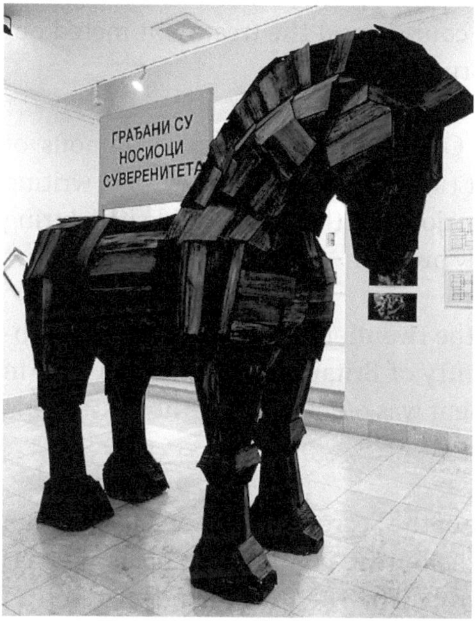

"Five months ago, Serbia started commemorating the victims of the canopy fall in the Novi Sad bus station by the 14-minute silence for the 14 victims. Around the country, Serbian citizens stood at main crossings, suggesting that 'Serbia has to stop'. This is in opposition to the government's clause 'Serbia must not stop' as the population holds them responsible for the tragedy due to its corrupt building deals. Occupying the public space in this spontaneous way demarcated months of the new territorialisation progressing into reclamation of the streets, buildings, parks and generation of the novel social environment which grew the national movement. Led by the students who started blockades at their universities considering that the population cannot continue until it cleans up our own backyard, Serbian residents walked out of their jobs and joined the young. The students are nominated for the Nobel Peace prize. The walking marathon with numerous actions followed across the country on a variety of important sites which is the subject of my artwork and its invisible timeline. I captured this historical moment by utilising iPhone photography."

Dr. Nela Milic, England

Not All The War Poets Were Anti-War

To go against the pro-war flow, even in poetry, took some nerves. To actually refuse to fight took real courage and the treatment meted out to consciousness objectors was brutal.

Siegfried Sassoon and Wilfred Owen are now the most famous of canonical poets of the Great War (1914-18). But when they were writing they were the odd ones out. The majority of the poems published during the Great War were bombastically pro-war.

During the first two decades of the twentieth century, poetry publishing was at its height. With the entry of Britain into World War One in August 1914, the British government was quick to enlist the best-selling poets and authors to help the war effort.

Charles Masterman was in charge of the Secret War Propaganda Bureau. Writers who produced work for the Bureau included the poets Thomas Hardy, Lawrence Binyon (who wrote 'For The Fallen', a poem still read at official Remembrance services today), Rudyard Kipling, Robert Bridges (poet laureate), and John Masefield. Other writers who wrote pro-war pieces for the Bureau included H.G. Wells, Arthur Conan Doyle, G.K. Chesterton, John Galsworthy and J.M. Barrie.

To go against the pro-war flow, even in poetry, took some nerves. To actually refuse to fight took real courage and the treatment meted out to conscientious objectors was brutal. Over 1,000 British conscientious objectors were imprisoned and 70 men died in prison due to mistreatment. They also earned the wrath of the pro-war poets.

A Christian to a Quaker

I much regret that I must frown
Upon your cocoa nibs
I simply hate to smite you down
And kick you in the ribs:

But since you will not think as I,
It's clear you must be barred.
So in you go (and may you die)
To two years hard.

We are marching to freedom and to love:
We're fighting every shape of tyrant sin:
We are out to make it worth
God's while to love the earth,
And damn it, you won't join in!

To drive you mad, as I have done,
Has almost made me sick.
To torture Quakers like a Hun
Has hurt me to the quick.
But since your logic wars with mine
You're something I must guard.
So in you go, you dirty swine.
To two years hard

We are marching to destroy the hosts of hate:
We've taken, every man, a Christian vow
We are out to make war cease,
That men may live at peace,
And, damn, you're at it now!

Harold Begbie

Harold Begbie (1871-1929) who toured the United States trying to whip up war fever, was far from the only poet at it. There was Henry Newbolt (1862-1924), he described war as being like a game of cricket. Jessie Pope

(1868-1941) also said war would be like a cricket match. William Watson (1858-1935) would be knighted for 'his patriotism in verse'.

Veritas Victrix

The Mill of Lies is loud,
Whose overseer, Germania's Over-lord.
Hath overmuch adored
The Over-sword,
And shall be overthrown, with the overproud.

Praised be the overwatching Heavens, that though
Falsehood her blare of brass may pitch yet higher.
Truth hath her trumpets also, and these of gold,
And she can blow
Longer than any liar,
Fronting the sun, high on her mountains old.

—William Watson, published in *The Times* 10 September 1914

Even if you don't know much about poetry, I think you will agree that is blooming terrible. The poets that have endured are the soldier poets —the poets who actually fought the war. Like Wilfred Owen who was killed in action on the 4 November 1918, just one week before the Armistice was signed.

Anthem For Doomed Youth

What passing-bells for these who die as cattle?
Only the monstrous anger of the guns.
Only the stuttering rifles' rapid rattle
Can patter out their hasty orisons.
No mockeries now for them: no prayers nor bells;
Nor any voice of mourning save the choirs—
The shrill, demented choirs of wailing shells;
And bugles calling for them from sad shires.
What candles may be held to speed them all?

Not in the hands of boys but in their eyes
Shall shine the holy glimmers of goodbyes.
The pallor of girls' brows shall be their pall:
Their flowers the tenderness of patient minds,
And each slow dusk, a drawing-down of blinds.

Wilfred Owen

Wilfred Owen was killed in action, on November 4, 1918, whilst supervising the crossing of a canal near the village of Ors, not far from the French/Belgian border. The telegram with the news of his death reached his parents Susan and Tom Owen in Shrewsbury as the bells were ringing in celebration of the Armistice on 11 November 1918. Wilfred Owen is buried in the village cemetery of Ors, in northeastern France.

As long as the organising principle of industrial society remains the preparation for war, then the words of Wilfred Owen will retain their power.

Phil Knight, Cymru/Wales

Knife Angel *by The British Ironwork Centre*

Knife Angel

'The expression on the Angel's eyes is one of sorrow, but also a challenge. He gazes out at us and asks: Why?'

The Knife Angel is a striking 27-foot-tall sculpture made from over 100,000 seized and surrendered knives.

Standing at 27 feet and weighing 3.5 tonnes, the Knife Angel sculpture is made from 100,000 confiscated or surrendered weapons, including blunted flick knives and kitchen knives, received from 43 Police Forces across the UK.

Conceived by Clive Knowles, the Chairman of the British Ironwork Centre, the aim is to raise awareness around anti-violence and anti-aggression. To create the sculpture, over 200 knife banks were created, with over 250,000 knives being removed from the streets.

Some of the blades were inscribed with the names of lost loved ones of the 80 or so families who have supported the project. Others were inscribed with messages from ex-offenders asking for forgiveness.

The construction took just over two years to create, with support from police forces, families affected by knife crime, and anti-knife crime charities. The Knife Angel undertook a National Anti-Violence Tour, with every host venue carrying out 30 days of intensive educational workshops and programmes.

The sculpture serves as a poignant memorial for those who have lost their lives to thoughtless acts of violence. It is also sparking national dialogue and educating youth on the dangers of violence, encouraging them to choose peace over violence.

Rebecca Lowe, Cymru/Wales

No More Knives

Knife crime is bad
And it's there at your door;
Please stop the killing
No more suffering any more...
It's a part of our society
One that should not be on our streets;

A statistic of life
One I hope not to meet.
Take away the heartache
and the strife;
No more families suffering
at the end of a knife...
It's time to make a stand
It's time to stop fear;
It's time for a culture change
This message is clear...

Let us all now unite
against this evil we face;
Stop this madness once and for all,
No more pain in this place

Knives are really senseless
Knives are really bad;
Knives destroy so many lives
and the freedom that we have

Take them right off our streets
Stop the tears and the pain;
Bring back peace to the people
Show them love once again,

No more blood spilt in anger
At the end of a knife;
They have no place in society
Don't destroy, give back life

Love is the answer,
Friendship is key,
A world without knives,
Now what a place that would be.

Derek Davies, Wales/Cymru

People say, what is the sense of our small effort? They cannot see that we must lay one brick at a time, take one step at a time. A pebble cast into a pond causes ripples that spread in all directions. Each one of our thoughts, words and deeds is like that. No one has a right to sit down and feel hopeless. There is too much work to do.

—Dorothy Day

9. NO JUSTICE, NO PEACE

Artwork: Tim Evans, Cymru/Wales.

Editor's Introduction: No Justice, No Peace

True peace is not merely the absence of tension; it is the presence of justice.

—Martin Luther King Jr.

In his book 'Where Do We Go From Here: Chaos or Community?' Dr. Martin Luther King Jr. described the triple evils of poverty, racism and militarism as forms of violence that exist in a vicious cycle. "They are interrelated, all-inclusive, and stand as barriers to our living in the Beloved Community. When we work to remedy one evil, we affect all evils."

It is impossible to talk of peace without talking about the things that cause its opposite, hence the ubiquitous protest slogan 'No Justice, No Peace'.

King himself used the same phrase in a letter to Willem Visser 't Hooft following King's receipt of the Nobel Peace Prize, and in a 1965 television appearance where he reaffirmed his call for an end to the war, stating: "There can be no peace in the world unless there's justice, and there can be no justice without peace. I think in a sense these problems are inextricably bound together."

The desire to live in peace is not the same as acceptance of conditions which are intolerable for a large sector of humanity. We cannot truly live at ease knowing that the richest 10 per cent of the global population owns 76% of global wealth. Or knowing that, across the world, people are still routinely discriminated against for the culture they are born into, their gender, race, sexuality, or the colour of their skin.

The question then becomes how we tackle such injustice in a way which challenges but does not perpetuate the cycle of violence—how we become the change we wish to see. This chapter aims to examine some of these questions.

War

Great War
Fantastic war
Splendid war
Wonderful war
Beautiful war
Patriotic war
Rational war
Justified war
Appropriated war
Legitimate war
Approved war
Valid war
Legal war
Political war
Devout war
Holy war
Callous war
Cruel war
Hard war
Greedy war
Grasping war
Vile war
Vicious war
Shameful war
Hateful war
Usual war
Standard war
Ordinary war

Enzo Marra, England

Imagine

Imagine you are made of straw
you are made of paper
you are made of string
you are made of glass
you are made of wax

You are able to be unmade
you are able to be undone
you are able to crumble
you are able to shatter
you are able to smash

You are just as frail fragile
as every other strange face
you see but don't see
you see through walk past

Image how anxious they could feel
imagine the small kindnesses
imagine the unobligated care
that only costs pocket of time

But don't just imagine it
enact it, make it lived, real

Enzo Marra, England

On Peace

Contrary to popular opinion
peace is not just
the absence of war,
after all you can sell weapons
when you are not fighting

True peace runs much deeper
past the skin, through the veins
and burrowing into the heart.
It's harmony in the social chorus,
serenity of the sacred stillness.

It's not just the quiet
that comes after the noise,
where everyone rallies
around their dead in a minute's
silence bathed in blood

It's reconciliation, justice
solidarity, a promise
of olives and doves
etched in to the memory
so deep it can't be removed.

Peace is not passive resistance,
It's a deeply affirmative act,
it requires repentance, regret
lest it trumpets again.

Johnny Giles, Wales/Cymru

Revenant

I work up this morning, I was not at all well,
My body was dead, my soul was in hell,
But something animated me from within,
Sharpened my teeth, stretched out my skin,
Drove me to seek out the flesh of the living,
When really I sought to be loving and giving,
I covered myself in carnage and gore
Found succour in violence, conflict and war,
Yesterday I was thinking of buying a shed,
But I'm spending the money on weapons instead.

Gareth Joseph, Wales/Cymru

Artwork: Tim Evans, Wales/Cymru.

Peace

Of course, when I first came across the term 'Criminal Justice System' I, like most people, failed to grasp the essential truth hidden in those three words. I understood from them, in my facile naivety, that the 'System' being described was one which provided 'justice for criminals'. I failed to realise that the Justice System is itself Criminal.

That enlightenment only came later after the Bridgewater Four, Cardiff Five, Maguire Seven, Guildford Four, Birmingham Six, Winston Silcott and others had served long sentences in prison for being innocent, having had their evidence distorted, ignored, beaten out of them or hidden by the CJS, the numbers naming each case hiding or abbreviating the agony and wrecked lives of individual innocent people. Or after yet others like Blair Peach and Joy Gardiner had died at the hands of the officers of the same CJS described in the phrase 'Criminal Justice System'—only then did I realise its true meaning.

By the time their counterparts across the pond had choked George Floyd to death while the homegrown variety had put peaceful protestors in prison for trying to prevent climate collapse or stop a genocide and I had experienced the joys of tear gas sprayed into a peaceful crowd daring to suggest a fairer distribution of wealth across the world, it had become clear: the Justice system was, itself, criminal—the Criminal Justice System.

You live and learn. I made a similar mistake when I first heard of the Ministry of Defence. Defence is fine—necessary acts to prevent yourself or another being destroyed or injured and no crime at all. Defence, as commonly defined, seldom entails dropping high explosives on unarmed civilians who are entirely without either the inclination or capacity to do you any harm at all but who happen to live near something you want. Usually that is called 'robbery with violence' or 'aggravated assault' but when done by the state in the name of our rich rulers it is called 'justifiable war', which is totally legal—or legal enough—

according to the laws made by the same or similar states acting on behalf of the same elite few, carried out by heroes and directed in their actions by those who talk loudly of their intention to bring peace to the world by diverting much needed funds from people's wages or services to sumptuously fund the arming of the defensive bombing raids.

Maybe that is what our rulers mean by 'peace': a lot of dead people who no longer object to what you want to do or try to keep what you are taking off them? It must be, as they gave the leader of the Stern Gang mob, Menachem Begin, who invaded a peaceful, multi-ethnic Palestine in 1948 to begin the Nakba which murdered tens of thousands, the Nobel PEACE Prize. Or maybe that was just their nice sense of ironic humour. The same sense that enabled them to support the ensuing regime of apartheid, murder and torture for the next seven decades while decrying those who dared to fight back as 'spoiling the peace' and was nothing to do with the oil fields of the region after all?

"Peace!" demanded the tyrant.

Was it 'peace' that brought down the Berlin Wall, won women's or workers' rights, overturned the plantation slave system, brought down the tyrants and apartheid? Or was it fighting back? Was it the nameless crowds saying no against all the odds and greater powers but fighting anyway until a win? Fighting for a better world for themselves and their children despite the very real risk this entailed of death and torture? Was Sam Smith, who led the final and greatest uprising to overthrow the British owned slave-plantation system in Jamaica which, though it failed and was suppressed with utmost cruelty, forced the rulers to have a rethink about the viability of said system—was he peaceful?

Closer to home and nearer in time—was it 'peace' or Michael Hickey on the roof of the prison, in midwinter frosts, fighting for justice, forcing the power of the state to be questioned which inspired a campaign which eventually sprang the prison cell, exposing the lies that had sent him down—when he could have sat in his cell in peaceful acceptance of the gross injustice visited on his young life—on all our lives? We all have that choice to make. Neither Sam nor Michael ever got medals or called heroes by the elite for their fights for justice: obviously they were the wrong kind of heroes.

Was it peace that wrung the welfare state from the trembling, unwilling hands of frightened rulers—where the peace brought by painkillers replaced the screams of the ill and dying in a more cruel world that had preceded the strikes, the marches, the defiance of the 1940s—the working class on the street showing a glimpse of our power—which forced the treasure chests to be opened and some shared—with education and housing made available together with the blessed opiates which previously had only eased the pain of the wealthy?

Peace is the feeling of belonging and oneness without stress, without rage or grief—not a possible state of being when there is no justice or even basic human needs being met and respected across the globe. Peace allows Life. Most of us crave peace—the fairness, the caring, the mutual support of community—but a very few crave the much greater piles of cash that can be made from war and those few are the ones making the rules so this world and its rulers take resources from the poor and the starving to spend on more and greater weapons of war guaranteed to make yet more desperate and starving—not deliberately, you understand, but just as a side-effect of the making of the great piles of coins in which the few roll—while having those arrested and criminalised who cry halt to the bloodshed for a fairer world, incarcerated for 'disrupting the peace'. It is a well-dressed, polite, well-mannered peace where 'the murmur of polite conversation drowns the screams from the cellar' (Alan Bennett, describing sighting the well-dressed mass murderer and torturer Pinochet, with his henchmen in a London restaurant during one of the General's visits to London as a guest of the British government).

Another side-effect is their bringing us another, bigger kind of peace: There are quite a lot of planets in the Universe apart from this one—but the others lack the turbulence and disorder, the chaos of life. Maybe that is why our rulers pursue policies and practices that bring huge profits and piles of coins but will guarantee an end to all that disorder, that untidiness, until this messy, life-laden planet spins more quietly in a derelict over-heated sterility—like all the others—in perfect peace?

See you on the roof.

Heather Booker, Wales/Cymru

No Peace With Reason—Socrates

A poet has reasons
that 'reason' can never tell,
believe me, Socrates.

In a dark time like ours,
some flood the streets,
some seek solace on their screens,

yet it's the internal
old movies we watch daily,
that make or break us—
often blurred, or cut,
with hardly any screen time
for your braggart: the Vulcan Spock.

Where is the brave
bright voice of 'reason',
when the armies of the night

raise their dark flags
on the decomposed remains
of old people, women and children?

Where is the law and order,
that you (or was it Plato?)
prattled about, would die for?
Where is the sterling republic,
that made you evict
the poet for the sake of it?

Where higher fences hit the headlines,
a passport's toxic noise
prevails, killing off all song.
While 'being autochtonous'
leads to Bibby Stockholms—
a legionella of biases, brazen lies.

Let rulers train
their imagination with poetry,
and memory with experience—
to shun avoidable bloodshed.
Whose r-word are you on about,
whose rabbit out of the hat?

Hasan Kahya, Cyprus/England

Revenge Is Off The Table

(*This poem was written in South Africa in late October, 2023*)

I sit in a country where apartheid was once the law, where apartheid
began a civil war.
I sit here while war begins in another country, where apartheid is an
accusation.
(But in this poem, where the weather is beautiful, revenge is off the
table.)

My grandfather, meanwhile,
As he fell from the sky, the B-24 exploding nearby,
quite clearly he saw the face of his 5-year-old daughter.
As he fell from the sky, his parachute upside down,
quite clearly he saw the green of the field.
As he fell from the sky, burnt hands clawing the chute open,
quite clearly he saw the hands of his wife.

I sit in a country where Nelson Mandela spent 27 years in prison, where
Mandela believed in forgiveness. So in this poem, revenge is off the table.

My grandfather, meanwhile
As he fell from the sky, quite nearly
he saw the old Black Walnut tree in the dry creek bed.
As he fell from the sky, quite nearly
he saw his brother and himself trapping ringtail.
As he fell from the sky, quite nearly
he saw the sheep grazing out in the pasture.

I sit in a country where 12 million are in dire need of housing but Nelson
Mandela believed in reconciliation. So in this poem, revenge is off the table.

My grandfather, meanwhile,
As he fell from the sky, and heard the crash of his plane, quite dearly,
he saw the faces of his crew.

As he fell from the sky, quite dearly,
he heard the song of the mourning dove.
As he fell from the sky, and landed in a tree, quite dearly,
he heard his own voice pray words that he'd forgotten.

I sit in a country where millions go hungry every day, but Nelson Mandela believed in the equality of all. So in this poem, revenge is off the table.

My grandfather, meanwhile,
After he fell from the sky, and met the faces of farmers brandishing
pitch forks,
quite clearly, he felt the solid ground beneath his feet.
After he fell from the sky, and witnessed German officers save him from
the farmers,
quite clearly, he felt his own heart beat strongly.
After he fell from the sky, and came face to face with the pilot who
downed his plane,
quite clearly, he saw himself standing on a hill, in a shower of radiant light.

I sit in a country where apartheid was once legal but Nelson Mandela championed peace and human dignity, and now people walk forward down the road. So revenge is off the table.
I sit in this country while in another country war wages in philosophies not in accord with Mandela's.

My grandfather, meanwhile,
after he fell from the sky, after he was a prisoner of war, after he was freed,
quite clearly asked God why he survived when so many didn't.

Years went by before he heard the answer.

You survived in order to practice believing
the weather is beautiful
and revenge is off the table.

Laura Grevel, Austria

This Is Not About Headscarves

This is me in this fading photograph.
It is early spring, circa 1966, in southwest Texas.
I was dressed by my grandmother. I am 5,
leaning against the sturdy trunk of a pecan tree,
wearing a pink sweater,
black-and-white hound's tooth trousers,
white socks, striped tennis shoes,
and a head scarf.

I am not a Muslim. I was not a Muslim.
But how quickly I forgot about our scarves!
In this photo, I am smiling at my Nanny,
who was the whipped cream of grandmothers.
I named her, when I was two, because she asked me,
what I'd like to call her—Grandmother, Grandma ... ?
I chose Nanny—out of the firmament, that name came.
A word that echoes that of so many other grans around
the world. I wonder how we know.

This is me, at 5. I am not a Muslim.
I am wearing a flowered headscarf,
arranged on my head and wrapped
around my neck, to protect me from
the elements, which in Texas, are strong
and sometimes adversarial.
In 1966 in Texas
many of my adult female relatives wore scarves—

my mother, my grandmother, my great-grandmother.
So did other American women, on into the 1980s,
to protect them, their hair, their faces,
from the sun, the wind, the cold,
the elements of life. It made sense.

This is me, now, over fifty years later,
remembering we used to wear scarves.
That it made sense;
that it was the style of the time.
We were Christian Texas women
who sometimes wore scarves in Catholic Mass too.

Forgive me, worldwide headscarf-wearing sisters,
that I ever felt a twinge of un-sameness
when I encountered a Muslim woman
walking down the street in a head scarf.
Forgive me that I forgot about that time
in Nottingham, UK, when I was walking
in the city wearing a black coat, black boots,
with my black scarf wrapped around my head
because the night was bitter cold.
And two times, white men
looked at me with a hate that
scraped my heart, took my breath.
I wondered why, till I thought, Oh!
Oh my! This is how it is.

This is me. I am sorry!
Forgive me, you friends of my daughter,
who wear headscarves, you two young women
who are among the friendliest humans
I have ever met.
Sisters, forgive my society
that so quickly forgets, builds a wall,
instead of a smile.
Forgets there is commonality of nannies,
a commonality of women,
a humanity that we must
never forget.

We must open our eyes.
My photograph is fading
but, clearly,
I see you there in the bombings
and the rubble, and
I will never accept this
I will not keep silent.
I will speak out in solidarity!

Laura Grevel, Austria

Cavalier

(Edited by Cam Black)

Foreign policy taxes democracy
Peace from the barrel of a gun
The horsemen ride
As economies cry
Demand and supply
Oil—well guarded
Fuel for votes
Politicians play king of a castle
Made from shifting sand
Population freed from oppression
Where only the dead remain
Pleas of peace
Soldiers at ease
When the horsemen sneeze
Death's odour drifts on breeze
Once oasis, now dead trees
Hear the people's pleas
Just release

Peace
Maybe this time
Dark horse roams the meadow
Rough diamond between its eyes
Hard lessons learnt
Hoof beats distract
Attract
White mare canters by
Peace in our world
Mane erects, follows
Gallops by side
Greets with a kiss
Love in our hearts.

Mick Mezza, Australia

Scripted Prayer

1 Ares

Why then Ares son of Zeus do you beat your drum calling upon friends to join a brutal bloc
Where Hades will encourage Orpheus to sing dirges of destruction.
You claim it is as your birthright to play your tune as all now will listen and not block.
We search for a cornucopia which we'll never find, to settle into an existence of harmony,
Look your birthplace it's burning, all that's left is charcoal for us to survey and you to mock,
Revel in your merriment as your message is being answered by those that will destroy,
As the wind carries your beat, the masses arise to the roar and others watch in utter shock

as mountains of funeral pyres create fumes where torrents of smoke flow in unilateral grief,
Whilst we pray to you to cease your playing and stop seducing the willing flock,
In utter devastation the living performs libations and the dead don't grieve.

2 Eirene

Well
then
Eirene you are opposite to your half-brother, carrying the sceptre for peace
The temples devoted to you are now empty where eddies of dust swirl
Your statues vandalised, cracked and strewn over the ground
Ares have you snatched your half-sister and hidden her so she could not be found?
Will your father send a hero to save our order from desertification into bountiful fields?
We pray to you, Eirene, to show yourself charming and graceful to take the lead
Show us a path so he can stop striking his drum and bring a halt to the battleground
Gather your flock with sweet tranquil harmonies where order can rise
Take his drum sticks and replace them with your sceptre
Present the olive branches, release the doves, bring on the feasts
For only peace will achieve a comfortable existence that unites us all
Where death will end, Orpheus will lay down his lyre
Ares will stop the beating and we will be pleased.

Mick Mezza, Australia

Levites

The blind can never describe colour
nor the deaf recognise an accent
for such things exist only in their imaginations
and unsensed dreams.
Few others can truly envisage
the visceral horror of blackened body parts,
dream the screams of the injured
begging a blind, deaf, God for death.
Taste the oil of grief hanging heavy in the air.

What of those who witness war
and drown the sound of sobs
with a waterfall of hollow words.
Judging themselves as blameless
as the deaf and blind.
Pleading confusion to justify inaction
with a shrug of their innocent shoulders.

The travails of a distant land
people whose foreign tongue entreaties
they can never comprehend
as if there were no context.
For if they admitted their witness
the guilt would forever stain their souls
and make Levites of us all.

R.M. Kain, Wales/Cymru

War

There are no truths allowed within any conflict.
Just the lies repeated to justify the savagery.
The old myths of good and evil,
of monsters, innocents and victims.

The disguise of self-interest analysed
by the beneficiaries at least one continent distant,
then repeated, and repeated, and repeated
in the media they control
until their narrative forms the only framework.

The millionaire arms dealers serving all sides
are never mentioned by name or company
far less numbered amongst the casualties.

Neither are the billionaire asset strippers
whispering in the ears of corrupt governments
to ensure their share of the regeneration spoils.

Even we far-away pensioners grow fat
as our investments in those global companies prosper.
All bribed to normalise the horrific events.

Only the tethered poor are killed, their homelands destroyed.
Hobbled by a lack of education, indoctrinated by religious bigots,
governments espousing the delusions of nationhood above humanity.

The twins of their neighbours kept in the same poverty,
the same ignorance, the same delusions
by the same people they are both dying to protect.

Neighbours denied the vision of their commonality,
neighbours whose first instinct would always be to help
if not for the indoctrination and lies.
justifying the madness infesting the battlefields.

Lies and lies and lies repeated in an endless loop
to distract them from evidence and reason.
There are facts, of course there are facts
but they will never be allowed to learn them.

The fact that the richest get even richer in every war ever fought.
That war is nothing but good business practice.
That sacrifice is necessary to fuel the division,
the hatred, the blame, the anger.

That those sacrificed are considered worthless
scapegoats under the bombardment
which destroys their meagre possessions, their ways of life.
All they treasure sacrificed for nothing but the same lies
they have been indoctrinated with their whole lives.

The lies told to stop us all considering the truth.
No child is ever born desperate to fight
they are taught that by those who profit
from every bloody war ever fought.

R.M. Kain, Wales/Cymru

No Justice, No Peace

I yearn for a world shaped by fairness—a society rooted in dignity, compassion and belonging. A place where every individual can stand tall in their own truth, unafraid, unburdened, unapologetically themselves. Above all, I long for Peace in the world—not as a distant dream, but as a living promise woven into the fabric of our daily lives.

I envision a Wales that is truly anti-racist in every sense—courageous in action, unwavering in principle. A Wales where people of every ethnic background share a common hope for a future that is inclusive, peaceful, accepting and richly embracing. A nation that becomes a radiant beacon of light to the world, stretching out warm and welcoming arms to the stranger, the excluded, the disadvantaged, the homeless, the marginalised and the refugee.

To become a genuinely anti-racist nation by 2030, as outlined by former First Minister Mark Drakeford, demands more than aspiration. It requires commitment—personal and professional—to a zero-tolerance stance against racism in all its forms. This must be visible in our words, evident in our behaviour, and steadfast in our attitudes. We must confront hatred, challenge prejudice and dismantle intolerance wherever it appears. For without justice, there can be no peace.

Ending racism begins with a simple yet powerful declaration: it ends with me. When each of us takes responsibility, when we stand firm and live that truth, transformation becomes possible. I call upon the people of Wales, the beautiful Land of Song, to lead with moral courage. Let us champion respect, fairness and social justice for all. Let us choose harmony over hostility, unity over division, and Peace in the world over conflict and fear. The time is now to safeguard the future for every child in our nation.

The killing of George Floyd shook the conscience of humanity, igniting one of the largest global movements for racial justice in modern history. Across Wales and beyond, voices rose together under the banner of the Black Lives Matter movement, demanding change that echoed across continents. The death of Christopher Kapessa in the Mountain Ash river, and the failure to secure accountability, remains a wound that cannot be ignored. Such moments remind us that justice delayed undermines peace denied.

Today, we must take a stand against racism in all its forms. Let us pledge—as individuals and as organisations—to build a society anchored in equality, dignity and lasting peace. Join the movement and make your commitment known through #ZeroRacismWales. Because when justice prevails, peace will follow, in our communities, in our nation, and across our world.

For more information visit www.zeroracismwales.co.uk

Uzo Iwobi, Wales/Cymru

Puppet Strings

Cheers whilst they gasp for breath,
Because they're the enemy,
Blinded by institutional mythologies,
Puppeted by the hands that feed,
Two sides to a coin,
That's all there can be,
Shadow and light cannot intertwine,
But can't they coexist?
Just as the tree has its rings,
The surface is only the beginning,
Following what you believe to be the light,
Can lead you to grow in strange ways,
Maybe instead of other,
We say together,
Acknowledging the difference in our roots,
Yet remembering our similarities,
No matter what we believe,
We grow from the same seed,
We all cry,
We all cheat,
We all smile,
We all bleed,
We're all the same breed,
Which nowadays is considered a radical philosophy,
Rather than a matter of simple biology,
Barriers constructed by golden finger tips,

Arming us with newly sharpened swords,
Delighted by the divide,
Shared smirks behind closed doors,
Whilst our blood stains the floorboards,
How quickly fear turns to war.
Now imagine what we could build,

If we unified arms,
Against the ring masters,
Attempting to keep us on leash,
One whole people,
United by understanding,
Who listen with empathy,
Who can finally see clearly.

Amber Berry, England

Wie Konnte Das Passieren?

We who have allowed
the return of evil
the return of those
who feel no regret in killing
while following orders
we who have allowed the frozen words
of our leaders
in shreds of half truth
to celebrate the murderers
of an entire population
in that strip of land
where there is no escape
How will we erase our sins
as history follows us
relentlessly
like an angry dog
with puzzled and
unsettling eyes
that keep asking
How could this happen?
Wie konnte das passieren?

Antje Stehn, Germany

Principles

Perhaps it is not easy
to suppress prejudice against
—another nation
—a different skin colour
—faith other than your own.

Perhaps it is not easy
—in the name of instilled principles—
to refrain from hatred or
executing death sentences
because they tell us it's okay,
or we think
that we have the right to inflict
—also mental one—
human pain.

It's worth
stopping and reflecting on the meaning of
such unworthy acts.
Awaking in oneself
love and tolerance,
replacing evil with good.
It takes more than pulling a trigger,
or in any other way destroying a person.

Eliza Segiet, Poland

(*Poems translated by Dorota Stępińska*)

The Pledge

Written as part of the Black Lives Matter movement, each individual, each poet, each artist gave a quote to The Pledge that honours Martin Luther King's 'I Have a Dream' speech. It also illustrates their commitment to combat social injustice and ensure the performance area they have is a safe one to create.

I Pledge:

1. To be an ally that that is true and hold the door for everyone who is at the back of the queue, as I will never truly know the weight of pain and the struggles they encounter. In the fight for equality, I will hold the door open for all those who are at the back of the queue in getting their basic needs and rights; it is the bare minimum I can do.
2. Black Lives Matter is the minimum expectation of globalism, no justice—no peace.
3. I pledge to help people and respect them the way they are.
4. I pledge to actively fight racism in all forms, comprehending the effects racism has on each individual, each family and on each community; respecting their feelings throughout.
5. I pledge to speak for equality, to fight inequality and celebrate diversity. For diversity is beautiful and can only make us a stronger society.
6. To live in peace is a basic right for every individual free from persecution and tyranny.
7. Each individual has the right to live in a warm safe environment and have warmth with food on their plates. Subsequently, appropriate medical provision should be available to everyone, whatever creed or religion.
8. I pledge to support the notion that every individual without exception has the right to respect and love. This journey can be taken together, hand in hand. I pledge to offermy hand, hope you will take it.
9. I pledge to always listen to people who say they are in need. To be less afraid to stand up to racism. To be less afraid to support those who are victims of any injustice. To be less afraid in a changing world, to deliver the spoken word in multiple languages and an array of colours

that reaches individuals across all barriers and all borders.

10. I pledge that the messages, the stanzas, the lessons of speakers, poets, publishers and teachers are delivered with pride and received with willingness to make it a kinder world

11. I pledge to use my voice to support those who have no voice.

12. I pledge to be a transmitter of moral values.

13. Poets to be loud and proud.

14. I pledge I will strive to treat all, as we would expect ourselves to be treated and to challenge those who identify others by the colour of their skin.

15. I pledge to choose every day to treat all humans with decency, ignoring preconceived ideas, and awakening to deep-seated unconscious conditioning that results in prejudgement of any behaviour afflicting and affecting others.

16. I pledge to give relief and respite to those who are in pain, unconditionally and respond with openness and with love.

17. Love is the pledge of trust and truth through all people, all minorities, all disabled people, all human beings have the right to live in dignity.

18. I pledge to keep Martin Luther King's dream alive so we may all one day soon realize the dream the Reverend envisioned, so that we could also dream of equality.

19. I pledge that, together we stand awaiting a new dawn to show us another day filled with hope. I pledge to show the direction of the light to those who just see darkness

20. I pledge to seek the truth, until everyone will see each other as equals under the law and under their God.

21. I pledge to speak the truth. I pledge to speak the truth to power, afflicting the comfortable and comfort the afflicted. I pledge to hold tight to the truth that words matter, recognising that the words we use fuel the actions, into spontaneous combustion, that ignite everlasting change.

22. I can't commit to being colour blind but I can commit to being kind until we learn to look inside. The mark of society is how it treats people; it's quite clear that treating people as a lesser human being is bullying,

it is anti-social and oppressive. I pledge to find a cure for colour blindness and help heal those who are too blind to see that equality fully doesn't exist.

23. I pledge to wash the slate clean and help those who don't have the means. I pledge to enable us all to have a strong spirit of love. I pledge to do better as individuals, and as a society to overcome the inertia.

24. I pledge to educate and to communicate so we can feel as one in light and love, to revel in the hope and joy of solidarity, so we can face up to the truth, to challenges we encounter. To follow the light and love.

25. I pledge every day to acknowledge the only way to pay homage to the struggle of our ancestors is to continue to fight for justice and relentlessly demand what is right, while people continue to be blinded that equality fully exists because it does not. Hence I never stop working for the equality our ancestors have sacrificed their lives for.

26. I pledge to use my voice for good. To decolonize my mouth. To speak with inclusivity. I pledge to walk the walk, humbly with courage, to match the courage of those being oppressed, holding up the universal laws of fairness, justice and love for all.

27. I pledge to hear stories from around the world and locations different from my own, for the benefit of others. I promise to hold and lift up high the everlasting beacon which guides the path to freedom.

28. I pledge to support the dream that one day healthcare will be prioritised above warfare, and invest the money on medicines that heal, instead of weapons that kill, resulting in our governments no longer selling weapons of mass destruction to oppressive regimes. I pledge to see everyone's worth, their potential, their grace, their light and shade.

29. I pledge that when I see any person of colour it would not define an individual by the colour of their skin. I pledge to treat all individuals with the same level of respect we expect to be treated with ourselves, regardless of age, race, gender or social standing.

30. I pledge not to be brainwashed by any media, but will have the decency to look through any mass prejudice and form my own unbiased opinion based on fact, rather than be submissive to herd mentality.

31. I pledge to celebrate that 'I am born of happiness, love and freedom.' I accept everyone with the same courtesy and compassion, so they can

fulfil their dreams for themselves and their families.

32. I pledge to support those seeking asylum, fleeing from famine, war and ethnic cleansing, thus an end to deportations, creating a borderless world. I pledge to walk the walk, in the footsteps of our ancestors in the march to glory, honouring the procession, by each forward step one of courage, that will never allow our bare feet to stop, the other foot with heart and compassion walk on towards a fair society, where barriers to everyday living are taken down from the Human Race.

33. I pledge not to judge a book by its cover whatever colour it is and celebrate its culture by dancing to the beat at every turn of the page.

34. I pledge that when asked the question, 'Why are they still fighting for civil rights? When are you going to be satisfied?' the answer I shall give will be, 'Never!' As long as ever black men, women and children in any time zone are living in the chalk lines of tyranny of the police brutality in the shadow of institutionalized racism, I pledge I shall never remain silent. Silence condones.

35. Though I may not know the experiences of those different from me, as we are all human, I pledge to listen. I pledge to be a part of the solutions rather than a spectator watching from the sidelines.

36. I pledge to remember my unearned privilege and perceived status, and to never assume I understand what life is like for those without the privilege I take for granted. I pledge by my actions to use our ability to communicate, our voices, our creativity as tools to combat racism. I will never be satisfied as long as there are victims of unspeakable horrors that are not humane, incomprehensible in any society.

37. I pledge that the dream must continue till we all live in harmony, I pledge to champion the fact that a heart beat is felt when love begins to grow.

38. I pledge to help the ignorant to understand that the origin of hate is fear. I pledge to show them a mirror and show them their reflection is not refracted but is true.

39. I pledge that I would enable each individual to practice their spiritual belief and put their prayer mat in the direction they wish without fear.

40. I pledge to peacefully protest in support of those whose status has

been marginalised by the minority.
41. I pledge to support individuality and leadership within communities, demand inclusivity, and help dismantle any authority that neglects to reinvest power in the people.
42. I pledge to resist discrimination and bigotry wherever I see it in the hope of a fairer world for everyone.
43. I pledge that no being shall sit on the ledge of despair, lacking the air of hope but float in the raindrops of growth that will create a forest of multicoloured flowers for all. I pledge that when each individual rises from being on one knee, they will all be blessed, feel blessed and bless their neighbour and their stranger. There will be no longer a black monopoly on pain and of lost hope. Together we rise in the throw of the dice. Together we rise to word prejudice into the archives, where there is no discrimination, no fear, an abolishment of hate forging a mix of races, beliefs and healthy debate. I pledge to fight injustice and racism through creativity, diversity and activism, showing solidarity with others against the forces of division.
44. I pledge I will consider it to be my moral duty not just to tick a like box when a witness to social injustice, I would seek to support the vulnerable and SAY IT LOUDER, so as not to champion the perpetrator.
45. This pledge will be shouted from the rooftops, preached from pulpits, learnt in our textbooks, stamped in our passports, placed next to every beat of my heart. I pledge to seek the truth, until everyone will see each other as equals under the law and under their God.
46. I pledge to always SAY IT LOUDER AND BE KINDER.

Created by Gary Huskisson, UK

Contributors:
India Stratton age 7, Theo Stratton age 10, Amber Kingston age 10, Mark Grist, Kelly Van Nelson, Cathy Carson, Fin Hall, Skylar J. Wynter, Ami Hoskins, Henry Jones, Joseph Seward, Greg Lamont, Marky Mark Symonds, Caroline Minter, Lantern Carrier, Landry Butler, Amy Hoskins, Rhoda Thomas, Polly Stratton, Umor Haque, Kezzamb, Jo Collins, Lesley Constable, Lucia Daramus, Rebecca Lowe, Si Fox,

Sameena Aziz, Margaret O Regan, Dane Ince, Franchesca Kirkpatrick, Michael Sindler, Hannah Roberts, Patricia Camp, Tim Evans, Christine Hall, Kizzy Wade, Des Mannay, Scott Coe, Generalissimo, Bryan Franco.

You can listen to The Pledge being read by its original contributors on YouTube, The Pledge: Poetry in the Brew.

Putting a price tag on peace and violence helps us see the disproportionately high amounts spent on creating and containing violent acts compared to what is spent on building resilient, productive and peaceful societies.

—Steve Killelea, founder and executive chairman, Institute for Economics and Peace (IEP)

Someone Told Me A Lie One Day

A poem based on the speech of MLK

Someone told me a lie one day
They made everything black and evil
It's always something degrading and low sinister
Black sheep, black list, black economy

Whereas white is always pure, high and clean
Even white privilege has a positive domain
Though the broadband is a broad church
We can fly the air like birds
Swim the seas like fishes
Walked in space to infinity and beyond
Yet in our humane development we are barely toddlers
As we can't walk the earth like sister and brother
Racial injustice is still the black man's burden and white man's shame
Wrongly incarcerated for 399 +1 years.
Innocent, presumed guilty
Racial injustice is still prevalent,
One must not get complacent,
GUILTY!
One must not get all Oscar Wilde, flippant,
The right to vote was hard fought for every citizen
Land was not given to make freedom relevant,
No health no wealth, no bus fare, no employment given
Just a reserved location on the bottom rung of the ladder,
Where lies the black politicians
Never faithfuls always traitors
Where once there was a black president,
Suited and booted as token representation
Replaced by an orange tyrant
Headlines and bylines, baby steps not strides
Are

First black this, first black that
First woman this first woman that
Where are the seconds, thirds, fourths and fifths?
Languishing at the back
Last.

Gary Huskisson, UK

Every gun that is made, every warship launched, every rocket fired signifies, in the final sense, a theft from those who hunger and are not fed, those who are cold and are not clothed.

—Dwight D. Eisenhower (1890-1969), US President and General.

I Run

Where we walk
we must march
Where we march we must run,
Run fast!

The black man have always had to run
Whether it is the Jamaican running under 10 seconds
Or the Africans running marathons
The black man have always had to run without dropping the baton.

Now I run out of my blocks towards their hate
Staring at hate directly into its eyes
Debunking their lies
I run

With the seas getting drier
And borders getting longer
Racial injustice is getting wider
Only the lies and mistrust are getting bigger
I run

I run
I run towards the Inconvenient Truth
The truth of how it is not what you think it is ...
My knee is sore and I cannot afford coconut cream anymore,
White like chalk,
The same colour drawn around another dead brother on the floor

I run Get back at ya, running down the right wing
The coaches and generals are bigoted and racist,
You may think it's getting better
If you believe that you are just as complicit
You are the ones who believe that finding out the truth

Is a waste of time
Believing in the avalanche lies is seen as a political compromise!

I Run towards an impossible ceasefire

Do you keep quiet, when the truth is not to your liking?
Do you change stations?
When someone from the global majority is dying
Do you think that they are all the same in Africa?
Black and got their breasts out on the front page of national geographic!

The killing of George Floyd was the day diversity stop breathing
It was the day racism tricked us all into thinking that everybody like you are caring
Now let me run up Capitol Hill
Giving the NRA the bill
For all the indigenous funerals,
And the constant banging of collective bargaining tables
I Run
You will see it on BREAKING NEWS; I run like the Black Forest Gump
Not stopping till I reach kingdom come
.. ..
I am pointing the remote control
And I point my hat(e)
In the direction of any oncoming hate and lies.
My Tom Tom Sat-Nav coordinates are set to RUN, RUN, RUN.
Each day I strut ahead of my shadow to bring down the reign of darkness, preparing for an avalanche of sadness.
I run
towards those purveyors of hate
who only believe that all truth is fake.
Instead of taking time to get to know each other—
positives and negatives,
negatives and positives—
through likes, reposts, and lost WhatsApp messages,

These faceless faces in balaclavas seek approval from meek strangers.
I am a man who walks with a white cane, but I know where to run.
I go on the B of the Bang
Don't look for the smoke
We are not choosing a pope

I RUN, I RUN, I RUN,

taking down their social media accounts,
roping-a-dope the rioters on their stolen scooters,
returning their bath bombs (lush!) and Sports Direct trainers

Watch me, like Ed Moses, hurdle over their barbed wire battle lines.
I will point my hat directly at their hateful eyes,
where I can see through their infinite lies.
My hat is signposted towards liars and fake news makers—
no intention to make them believers; I intend to make them listeners.

I RUN, I RUN,

I RUN towards their spineless faces, avoiding their leftover faeces.
I will point my hat in the direction of their petrol bombs and incendiaries.
I run to extinguish their hotel fires, throwing over a blanket of kindness
to wipe out all their blindness.

In my holster, a black pen and white paper
And for dutch courage a 10-year-old gold fiery whisky.
I arouse the underbelly of humanity.
They have nothing to lose or gain;
Whatever they choose, they will have unrivalled pain—
stricken by poverty, lost in austerity.

Their head, heart, and hands are the forks in the wheel, turning mourning into dancing,

unmarked graves into blossoming gardens.
They smile with broken teeth, just to annoy the white elite.

I RUN, I RUN, I RUN.

I point my hat to the start of every rainbow, where I stand tall in spite of any adversity.
Though my disability has no visibility,
I will remove the barriers to gender and race equality.
I am clear that I will stand by anyone who has any mental insecurities.
We are still divided in so many ways.
Life will never be the same...

Red hot iron, burning shop window frames
An iron that once branded me with my slave owners' name
Such presidential terms always end with insurrection and NRA candle flames.

I RUN, I RUN.

Let me adjust my hat(e), so I am not blinded by the sun.
No one can stop me going on the B of the Bang.
I will run through the shadow of death, chasing the Proud boys and the EDL all the way
down to their
HE double L HELL.
While the right-wingers are defecating on community walls,
I'll be reading Romans from this week's best seller called The Bible.
They must refrain from exploiting foreign residents, for you yourselves, in the name of freedom:

If your enemy is hungry, feed him; if he is thirsty, give him something to drink. Don't let evil conquer you but conquer evil by doing good.

—Romans 12:19-21

Not available on X

I RUN, I RUN.

With my branded hat, I will stand on top of the podium.
I will be standing like Smith and Carlos, shoeless with impoverished black socks,
a black scarf around my dry neck to commemorate those who were lynched
and a prayer for all those thrown overboard in the Middle Passage
As my national flag raises, I will raise my black-gloved fist high up in the sky
and loudly sing my anthem:

WE SHALL OVERCOME.

For freedom,
I run for freedom.
I run; we shall overcome.
My mental disposition has me living a passion.
One must come close to death so I can face this life's conundrum.
They must not exploit or oppress a foreign resident, for themselves were foreigners in this
human race for freedom.
Each breath is a breath of a death dodger of 100-year-old James Baldwin,
taking an honourable man to run for freedom.
Time to confront the ugliness of the right and reference it as light.
On your marks,

GET SET,
WE RUN, RUN, RUN.
GO Start eating the cats and the dogs

Gary Huskisson, UK

Fasc-isn't

Democracy dying or dead?
Just a Spandau Ballet?
The Iron Curtain threatens,
Between Dover and Calais.
A New World Disorder!
They invade borders!
They rename water!
Propped up by the sickest hoarders—
They want you to never make it!
They want to find your dough and rake it!
They want to acquire your soul and rape it!
They sell racism. They peddle hatred!
A mental prison for millions of people,
'Awake' but asleep in a vision of evil!
Millennial hope?
A glimmer in the distance.
Verging on an unthinkable existence!
The near future is uncertain,
World is run by bastard schisms,
Over time—what is certain;
The way of fascism, it isn't.

Gareth Twamley, Wales/Cymru

Globalise This!

We can American anything!
Isn't Amazon amazing!

Why go through life wanting?
Or waiting?

Iphones! Ipods!
Imacs! Iwannadies!

Can we globalise peace?
Can we globalize hunger?
if we give up
Prime, McDonalds and
Coca-Cola?

Alan McGuire, UK/Spain

Certain Men, Abject Hell

Obstinance, obstinance.
Certain men start wars,
unleashing vile plagues upon the generations,
failing to listen to their own failings
failing to listen.

Unable to comprehend humility,
stubborn in ego and idiocy
they proliferate worn out prejudices
refusing to imagine, to consider for one moment,
maybe things have moved on.
That people are talking and listening
across borders,
natural or constructed
embracing the wonders and concerns of our world together.

But no,
holding onto high office and keys of media empires
these maniacs of war enjoy too much the mischief of division,
trashing language
perverting truth,
that they
spin and spin
constructing narratives to maintain
their bloated lives within gated echo bubbles
where the sycophants, the enablers, with eyes on a prize,
have neither the wisdom, the wish or wit to say,
calm, listen, think.

And so,
the tragedy of their mean inchoate designs, unfold.
Young men and women, conditioned or coerced
do these dirty dogs' foulest dealings,

pulling triggers, pushing buttons, touching screens
that drop
bomb after bomb,
on schools, on hospitals, on shopping malls, on cafes, on playgrounds...
where mothers and fathers will lose children
and children will lose mothers and fathers.

And as the grey and ochre dust lingers,
clinging to the blood of dazed figures, who,
emerging from sudden tombs,
drag their broken bodies through twisted metal and tearing flesh rubble
reaching to and from decimated lives and loves,
coming to terms with being barely half alive
wishing it was them dead too.
Cities, towns and neighbourhoods,
favourite places to hang out, to runabout or simply sit and watch the
world go by,
are now just mounds.
The 'memories of childhood'
are now just mounds
of blasted cement, torn fabric, shards of metal and glass
under the
dust and dust
that suffocates the skeletal spectres of home.

(*In response to Simon Tisdall in* The Observer *15.10.23*)

Tim Davies, Wales/Cymru

10. FOR PEACE AND PLANET: CLIMATE CHANGE AND PEACE

Editor's Introduction: For Peace and Planet—The impact of Climate Change

'We are the first generation to feel the impact of climate change and the last generation that can do something about it'
—Barack Obama

Climate change is the gravest and most urgent crisis facing humanity, and its effects will have a lasting impact on global peace and security.

Since the Industrial Revolution, global temperatures have risen by 1.2°C, leading to more frequent and severe weather events like heat-waves, floods, and storms. These events threaten lives, ecosystems, and economies, and become harder to manage over time.

Climate change disproportionately affects the poorest communities, indigenous peoples, and future generations—those least responsible for the crisis. While countries have pledged under the Paris Agreement to limit warming to 1.5°C, current actions fall short, potentially pushing temperatures up to 2.7°C by 2100.

These extreme weather events endanger people's lives and livelihoods, wildlife and nature. Warming beyond 1.5°C means that critical environmental tipping points, such as the widespread dieback of the Amazon rainforest, become more likely and could lead to irreversible damage.

Despite the grave nature of this threat, we are woefully under-prepared for what is to come. A report released last year by the Global Center on Adaptation (GCA), which took contributions from 18 nations including the UK, described the preparations made to deal with climate change's effects as 'gravely insufficient'. It declared that further inaction would result in poverty, water shortages and soaring levels of migration, with an irrefutable toll on human life.

Trillion-dollar investment is needed to avert 'climate apartheid', where the rich escape the effects and the poor do not, but this investment is far smaller than the eventual cost of doing nothing. The greatest obstacle, says the report, is not money but a lack of 'political leadership that shakes people out of their collective slumber'.

Climate change represents a threat to global security. Specific risks include scarcity of resources, food insecurity, forced displacement due to climate-related disasters, and increased inequalities, with women and other vulnerable groups being disproportionately affected.

Tackling the spectre of climate change will require governments and countries to think beyond their own borders and consider the long-term global impact of their actions.

> *Our country is committing infanticide, genocide, the looting of nations. I'm determined to be there until they kill me. How much longer will that be?*
>
> —Brian Haw, peace campaigner

Let The Planet Heal

As we look at history we see wars
Stretch back forever and so frequently
There are far too many wars still raging to list
Humankind is motivated by greed, aggression and
Coveting other people's territory
When really this is nonsense,
How can anyone own the earth, the land?
It belongs to the planet and will be there
Forever, long after Humankind has ceased to exist
They will disappear just like the dinosaurs did
But unlike the dinosaurs, who had no fault
And caused no harm to the planet
For the extinction of our species, we will be to blame

We recycle conscientiously, every bit of plastic,
Glass, cardboard and far more, we do this to help our world
To what effect when bombs and rockets blast away
Destructively round the globe every day?

We must rid ourselves of the aggressive warmongers
Rid ourselves of the Governments so full of aggression
Get rid of those that want to fight to gain territory
Our species needs to be free of such
We must strive for peace
For the protection of life
And of our planet

Peace must be our goal
It is monstrous that we cannot feed our people,
Have enough clean water for them to drink,
But we can easily afford weapons
It is a vast failure of Capitalism
That war is such a source of profit

To make those already rich even vastly richer
And those who finance it and profit
Run no risk of injury or death

War must cease
Peace must bloom
And we must make this happen
Otherwise, we are doomed.

Richard Harries, England

2525

I got up
Drank Actimel
Washed the tiny tin foil top
And washed the little plastic bottle
I recycled both
Caring
Wanting to do my tiny bit for the planet
To be green

Then turned on the news
War in the Ukraine, plane crashes with hostages aboard
Violence between India and Pakistan
Israel bombing Palestine
Trouble between Iran and Iraq
UK and USA bombing Yemen
So we are at war just not saying so
So we can afford a bombing campaign
But no social services support
Or even potholes repairs, and so much more
This could indeed be a long poem

With Artemis the USA continues to fund
Vastly expensive space programmes
While also have little social care support
And folk going bankrupt if they dare to get ill

World leaders flying in jets to conferences
About reducing carbon emissions
And in the case of Withernsea's MP Graham Stuart
Makes a 6,313 mile round trip to vote for the Rwanda Bill
Making around 2 tonnes of carbon emissions on the trip
He was in Dubai for the COP28 conference

Volcanoes erupt, fires get out of control
Fracking continues to disturb the planet for profit
Flooding is everywhere
Coastal erosion continues unabated

What use are our efforts to be green and recycle
If humankind carries on as it is?
With the greed of nations and governments
With massive wars, no peace
Deforestation of the Amazon rainforest
The fires there uncontrolled
With greed for minerals and power
Greed for other's territory
Then the future looks bleak
I will still recycle
I just don't know why

A song asked if mankind will still
Be alive in the year 2525
That was in 1969
And nothing has changed in the way
Humankind treats the planet and each other
And vastly increased technology has made

Things far worse
What the fuck are we doing?
The wars to end all wars did no such thing
Peace, we need peace.

Did no one listen to Joni Mitchell, Bob Dylan, Tom Paxton
Nina Simone, John Lennon and so many more?

Does anyone think we are not on a road to disaster?
Does anyone think the little we can do to be green
Will make an iota of a difference?
The planet will survive certainly
Unless we actually blow it up

But once we have exterminated our own species
Like we do so many others
The world may be a better place
The only way we can help ourselves and survive
Is to find peace.

Richard Harries, England

Wartime Blooms

Imagine change as a garden—
Dahlias, Orchids, Tulips thrive
under the shadow of the Second World War,
then wilt when peace arrives.

Beside them, Irises, Daffodils, Peonies—
Resilient, stunning black Roses,
bloom amid falling bombs, fade
as battles cease. In brief, harsh seasons,
change emerges, shattering barriers.
War-time Wildflowers, as if crafting ships
from stardust, for warriors in strife.

Each stands as a testament
to unwavering resolve
Embodying Mother Earth, they birth bravery—
the sun revives the weary, the moon guides the lost.
Their worth, undeniable,
shines through day and night—they did it all.

Longing for someone to miss them, to notice
their absence. Women are strong
like roots—beautiful like flowers.
Has Mother Earth ever called for conflict,
or does she weep for each fallen petal?
How many times has the sun
smiled at a bomb?
How many times has the moon
wanted to shine on a battle? Consider
our war-time deeds, how we turned into
camouflaged Carnations.
If armistice Asters can make gardens rise
from war's rubble, why can't we be the change?

Stephanie DuPont, USA

Herd Of The Waves

She sits in a land unkind   only friend a picture of her son.

I watch her weathered hands
over the open flame
camellia sinensis swirls in the pot
making chai to tell her story.

Sage burning on the puja tray   the sea is an indifferent mother.

The hopeful waves
betrayed and stole her son,
when immigrating
to live a life worth living.

She holds a marigold   crushes it in her palm.

heavy eyes follow the steam as it rises
look into mine
sings the lines

Beti, life is as precious as marigold
and some will never bloom.

inside she remains
a mother.

Do You Feel?

Do fungi feel?
Do they revel in their rise
or does the weight of warming skies
drown their fragile fruiting bodies.

When I forage in the moors,
I ask the oak tree
does it mind growing the beefsteak?

I ask the decaying leaves
do they mind feeding the fairy ring?

I ask the soil
does it mind protecting the mycelium?

I deepen into the moors
clouds of damp
blankets of lichens
greet slow slugs
gift silver birch
words of tenderness.

I ask the Earth

Do humans feel?
Do they cherish their climb
or does the weight of ego
drown what they claim to love.

Manisha Dhesi, England

Interdimensional

I spent the night crying
only me and the moon
she told me to stitch my eyes to my feet
I ate a star
looked a little deeper
saw life moving beneath
moss spreading across
lesser celandines bright star on the ground
red-seeded dandelions chasing the wind
snails creating homes to be swallowed by the soil
a man searching for me in him
he kisses my brown eyes
to get the mycelium power
it was past metaphysics
beyond pataphysics
it was interdimensional.

Manisha Dhesi, England

Shore

Light going, on the shore
of evening: distance blurs; the air itself
is going granular
like a gust of dry seeds, a fall of dust
from the Sahara. Colours
too are crumbling, through the greyer
undertones of blue,
ash-lavender, Prussian, Delft, old cobalt,
towards indigo. The stub
of a day worn down, re-sharpened
until it's too little to hold...
Night falls, words say, but it's a rising,
like a tide coming not in
but up through the shingle,
a glint of it here,
there, all around you... the way drought
loses its grip by darkening
in gullies, tyre ruts, craters, with the memory,
the smell, of water...
as sleep you can't lay hold of must forget
itself to be. Blue, blue-
grey, on the edge of evening, and distinctions
blur; you could fear
it's your eyes failing, before night vision,
more like touch than seeing,
comes... It waits, like sleep, like peace,
for us to trust it,
always out of, almost within, reach.

Philip Gross, Wales/Cymru

11. WAYS FORWARD—OUTPOURINGS OF HOPE

Three Doves by Bob Starrett

Editor's Introduction: Positive Peace

'Hope is the one good god remaining'

—Theognis of Megara, 6th Century BCE

Hope is our best weapon—for want of a better word—against a world which constantly tells us that war is inevitable, that we may as well not bother working for peace. In the face of a cynical world, hope is all we have. Hope means placing our faith in each other and our collective ability to re-imagine the world in which we live, to create new and better ways of living together.

Creating peace demands collective action. We need to look beyond our own individual interests, to go beyond competitive aggression and consider how we might work together—across nations, across borders. This is more important than ever at a time of impending global climate crisis.

The Institute for Economics and Peace (IEP) coined the term Positive Peace to describe the attitudes, institutions and structures that create and sustain peaceful societies. Positive peace extends beyond the mere absence of conflict—it considers what is required to create a fairer, equitable society, in which conflict is no longer required.

The Eight Pillars of Positive Peace are: well-functioning Government, a sound business environment with economic security, equitable distribution of resources, acceptance of the rights of others, good relations with other countries or between ethnic, religious and cultural groups, free flow of information and a free and independent media, a high standard of education, and low levels of corruption.

A peaceful society is one that works well for everybody. Positive Peace does not just reduce a country's risk of conflict, but can also help improve many other social factors, including governance, economic development, well-being and ecological performance. Hope, then, is not just a noun, but an active verb. By using the model of Positive Peace we can build more peaceful and sustainable ways of living, creating more peaceful nations—and ultimately a peace-filled world.

'Peace Gives Us A Chance'
Photographed by Steve Huenneke at
SIPTU College, Custom House,
Dublin, January 2024.

Peace Gives Us A Chance

I flew from Frankfurt, Germany to Dublin on January 18. My flight was delayed exactly two hours because of a snow storm. If it hadn't been snowing in Frankfurt, and my flight was on time, I could not have got this picture. I would have taken the train to Wexford and never seen this scene. But I arrived too late to take the train, so I took the Wexford bus instead.

I had arrived on a rare, cold, bright sunny day in Ireland. If it was cloudy as usual, the sky over Dublin would not have been blue. It was so blue. The blue sky added something intangible to the picture. It spoke—it speaks—of hope. As the Wexford bus was slowly rumbling through heart of downtown Dublin, I took this photo from the window of the bus as it was moving.

If the previous stoplight had been longer, the bird would not have showed up at just the right time as I passed by. The Wexford bus (which I happened to be riding) and the bird did not just meet up anywhere —they met up in front of SIPTU College—this building is about the closest thing Dublin has to a skyscraper. A skyscraper with a sign so large it covers six stories of the building.

If the SIPTU College building—with its sign—was not there, the bird would not have been in the right place. SIPTU College has faculty, staff and students with a conscience, so they erected this sign on the building—weeks before I arrived that day.

So, this photo was the work of many people—I cannot just claim it as my own. I recognise each and every one of them. If all those people at SIPTU College did not have such a conscience—or if they did, but still just lacked enough gumption—there would be no sign there. The bird and the tall building coming together there would have meant nothing special at all. I would probably have just deleted the photo, if I had bothered to even take it. And I will tell you in this world of artificial intelligence and what not—this photo is real. It is not fake. I ask you to trust that and to believe me. If there is no trust and truth, peace is hard. It all comes down to a choice.

Did you just think the same thing I did? Yeah, but if only. If only the bird would have been a pure white dove instead of a common dirty seagull, that would have made the story of this unlikely picture—and the picture itself—really perfect. The pure white dove is the symbol of peace. Seagulls are not. Is it possible we don't give peace a chance, as much as peace gives us a chance?

Peace must be screaming at us! "I went through all this work to send you a sign, a sign of peace. A sign for peace! The sign is right in the picture—there it is! The bird? What about it?" Okay, everything is not just as it should be. People, you were not born without any imagination. Maybe the final piece of this peace sign is just that—peace requires your imagination, as well as your human sympathy and your horror of war. Go full John Lennon here. Imagine it's a dove. If you have an imagination and can see this chance—or any other opportunity—which I, Peace, have presented to you, don't wait. Act.

Steve Huenneke, Ireland

Wales As A Nation Of Peace

"At a time of unprecedented global tensions, Wales has a unique opportunity to champion the cause of international peace."

—Derek Walker, the Future Generations Commissioner for Wales

A report from Academi Heddwch Cymru, Wales's national peace institute, outlines the potential for Wales to become a Nation of Peace.

The report sets out how Wales can and should aspire to become a Nation of Peace—in order to establish itself as a globally responsible nation, to raise the profile of Wales internationally, to build stronger communities within Wales, and because peace has a value in its own right. Key findings include:

Peace is more than the absence of war. It is about creating a better world through societies living without fear, it is building social resilience alongside individual rights, and it is about promoting social justice, fairness, respect and equality. This is what is known as positive peace. A number of states have made conscious decisions to place peace firmly on their national agendas, making peace part of their national identity and a key value for which they are recognised. Peace is seen by these states as something which evolves as part of a national dialogue, and its hallmark is the manner in which they conduct their relationships.

Becoming a Nation of Peace is in everyone's interest. It will significantly enhance Wales's international profile as it has for other 'peace nations', and provide Wales with a distinct identity on the international stage. Becoming a Nation of Peace will have a positive impact on how Wales governs itself as a devolved nation with diverse communities and interests. Above all, however, Wales and its government should promote peace because peace has a value in its own right.

A strong foundation exists for Wales to become a Nation of Peace. For more than a century, the people of Wales have undertaken innovative—sometimes world-leading—initiatives to promote peace. With devolution, the scope for further innovation and a clearer identity as a Nation of Peace has vastly increased for Wales. Legislation and policies such as the Well-being of Future Generations (Wales) Act (2015) and the commitment to net-zero demonstrate that the Welsh Government is capable both of innovation and visionary leadership with transformational potential.

Peace involves the whole of society. Despite significant progress towards 'positive peace', much still needs to be done. Wales's identity as a Nation of Peace will not only be about the narratives we relate, though these are important, but also about what we do and how we do it. It will be about how relationships are conducted, about using dialogue as a way of life, about being open to different perspectives and beliefs, and about seeking cooperation rather than conflict with others whether they are like-minded or not.

Gaining 'Nation of Peace' status will not just be about a series of policy initiatives for Government to enact and targets for it to reach, but a direction of travel which involves the whole of society including local government and civil society organisations—many of which are part of broader international coalitions and make significant contributions to peace.

International outlook

Although the UK Government has reserved powers on foreign, defence, security and international development policy, there is still scope for the Welsh Government to act internationally. The Welsh Government has powers over education and culture, both of which can be used to establish dialogues and promote peace, as well as the ability to add its voice to global debates. It has also provided practical support for international development such as the 'Wales and Africa' programme, while its 2019 Refugee and Asylum Seeker Plan, which aims to establish Wales as a 'Nation of Sanctuary', demonstrates how innovative thinking can create opportunities to act internationally.

Wales's international activities are not limited to the Government in Cardiff. Civil society organisations, including the peace movement in Wales, universities and schools (especially through the Taith programme) all have opportunities to act internationally and can play a role in promoting peace.

Peace Goals

Following the example set by the Welsh Government's seven Well-being Goals, the report suggests that Wales should have Peace Goals which would have a legislative basis similar to that of the Well-being of Future Generations (Wales) Act (2015). The details of these should be developed as part of a national conversation leading to a National Manifesto for Peace. The report can be found on the Academi Heddwch website atwww.wcia.org.uk/academiheddwch/

About Academi Heddwch Cymru

Academi Heddwch Cymru is Wales's national peace institute and is the first of its kind in the four nations of the United Kingdom. It belongs to a global family of peace institutes that bring together expertise to serve with the common aim of using peace-rooted approaches to global challenges.

It was established in 2020 as the result of a twelve-year campaign by civil society groups following the suggestion that Wales might become home to a new military academy for the UK. The Chair is the former Archbishop of Wales and Canterbury, Dr. Rowan Williams. In 2022 Academi Heddwch was awarded long-term strategic funding to support development of the Welsh Government's international strategy through fostering relationships across academia, research and peace sectors internationally.

Academi Heddwch aims to extend Wales's long-standing tradition of peacemaking and peace-promotion by developing and coordinating an independent community of researchers in related fields. Funded by the Welsh Government but independent, Academi Heddwch works to place peace firmly on Wales's national agenda as well as on the international stage.

Mererid Hopwood, Wales/Cymru

Wedi Cad Coludd Ar Ddrain

Cynddelw Brydydd Mawr, the twelfth century poet describes the battlefield with this line: 'Wedi cad coludd ar ddrain'—'after the battle, I saw entrails on thorns'. Hundreds of years later, we seem to be none the wiser...'

I should like the words 'alien' and 'foreign' to be banished from the language. We are all members of the same family."

—Charlotte Despard

The wind that shakes the memory tree wakes me.
It tears the flesh from the carcass of the mare that rides my night,
And howling, hurls it, skin and meat,
to dress the wounded branches, furious fright,
beside the entrails of my brother,
my father, my sister, my mother.
For there is no foreigner
no alien, no other.
This is the mercy of memory.
And then before me, bold, bright,
dawn's first blade slits the day open—
and unforgotten
the tree now sliced with light's clean knife
shows me how it grieves for the leaves of life.

(For Charlotte Despard, see *To End All Wars*, Adam Hochschild, p. 279
Cynddelw Brydydd Mawr: a 12th Century Welsh poet—the line translates: 'After battle I saw entrails on thorns' ... see, alas, similar descriptions of WWI battlefields in Hochschild's book.)

Mererid Hopwood, Wales/Cymru

Rhyfel

Mewn ymateb i 'Rhyfel' a 'Blotyn Du' Hedd Wyn

Gwae ni pan gaeo'r pum pelydryn haul
yn ddwrn dan gysgod storm, pan waedo glaw
y bore naddion dur heb adael traul
ar ddwylo'r duwiau, dim ôl chwys na baw;
gwae ni pan glatsho cwyn cleddyfau'r gwynt
ym mhennau'u mamau nhw a'n byd ni'n gân,
a hiraeth hardd yr hen delynau gynt
yn suo crud ein holl freuddwydion mân;
gwae ni am hawlio'r sêr a'r lleuad bell
a'r cwmwl aur sy'n cylchu'r glesni maith,
gwae ni am sarnu'r Drefn, er gwybod gwell,
a byw heb weld y cynrhon yn y graith;
gwae ni, gwae fi, am fod yn rhan o'r set
sy'n gwneud dim byd ond 'fire and forget'.

Mererid Hopwood, Wales/Cymru

War

In response to Hedd Wyn's 'Rhyfel' and 'Blotyn Du'

What mercy when the sun's five rays of light
shut tight and rain in fistfuls splintered steel,
when storms and shadows leave no trace of fright
or sweat on bloody hands that do not feel?
What mercy when the winds are swords so sharp
their terrors lash out grief in mothers' heads,
while still we cradle dreams, and sing the harp's
sweet *hiraeth* having torn the world to shreds?
What mercy when we claim the moon, the cloud
with bands of gold, the sky and every star,
and dress the Order as we knew it in a shroud,
oblivious to the maggots in the scar?
Let pity weep for me, for us, the set
that does no more than 'fire and forget'.

NOTES

One of the RAF missiles is called 'Storm Shadow' and the name of this method of distance killing is 'Fire and Forget'.

Mererid Hopwood, Wales/Cymru

A Peaceful World

A world in disarray
In desperate need
Of hope
And change
A world plagued
By hatred
By injustice
And bigotry
But it does not
Have to be that way
Try kindness, rather than cruelty
Try compassion, rather than judging
Try love
Love one another
Differences and all
And see how far
WE go.

Davion Moore, USA

National Defence

I think a lot about national defence and the fact we are so beholden to the need to procure resources outside of the UK, fossil fuels or otherwise. I am familiar with the argument for global capitalism, that global interdependencies foster positive networking and drivers to avoid war. However, I think in our time that argument becomes more spurious each day, let alone the false premises upon which it was founded.

For the UK, the best way to ensure national defence and integrity is to foster a self-sustainable domestic economy. This is not a proposal to withdraw from global trade networks but rather to acknowledge drivers for war, particularly hybrid warfare, of which we are extremely vulnerable to. So, what prevents us from shifting to an economy that results in better national security?

The answer is certain individuals and the corporations they have significant stakes in. Some of those people profit from war and the UK being in a permanent state of anxiety, when it comes to national defence and security matters. What is more, and what is incredibly sad and depressive, is that said individuals are British nationals!

The question becomes, then, how to convince them? How to accommodate them and to give them a slice of the pie of the visionary economies and modes of living we wish to see built and enabled in the UK? These are the leading political and social questions and problems for our time, and we'd better quickly begin to solve them.

I've also been thinking a lot about domestic national security matters too, and which dovetails over to my citation of 'hybrid warfare'. So, I'd like to mention a few things here and particularly given the MI5 Chief's recent talk about budget restraints.

As we see adversarial foreign powers engage more and more in domestic matters covertly, through criminal gangs as well as the usual spy and sabotage stuff, we've also seen the trend to do 'culture war'. That is, to deploy data processing tools and visualisations to identify issues and people to influence, to increase the probability social strife, conflict and division ensue. I know a lot about that as that was at the heart of my PhD in the early 2000s.

This has meant budgets to tackle domestic extremism, the far right in particular and as is my concern, have been slashed. The thing is, such groups are likely to be used as proxies in that more sophisticated digital culture war. That aside, the problem remains on how to, within budget, lower the domestic extremist threat. The answer? That can be found in the tools to wage social and cultural warfare except here, taking a more angelic approach.

What do I mean by an angelic approach? Statistical analysis is advanced here, and we can actually chart the life course of individuals and groups and determine who is likely to travel to the threshold of extremism, and thus intervene. One of the statistical plots is an 's shape' graph and the point of inflection, steep. We have to get off graphs like that and become more nuanced and intervene, at earlier stages.

Rather than tip said people and groups into an action (a set up) and swoop on in, which has been the traditional approach and incredibly costly, it is far better to intervene earlier. I know, I would have to do a proper cost benefits analysis but intervening early, given how accurate said statistical projections now are, is likely to be more cost effective, more ethical and have other added benefits.

In short, become more angelic and have people engage with said 'marks' early on and in a kind way. I do not mean send in social services, God forbid, but rather a soft and gentle nudge approach where opportunities are given and that are suited to said individuals. Such a method is particularly suited to those who are nationalists or have strong British identities. Those on the path to extremism here are crying out for engagement and belonging.

So, what would a case story be like here? Say, from identification to initial intervention and the extended work then needed? Ah, now this would be to overstep the boundaries on what are pressing and very real national security matters. What I can say, though, is taking an angelic approach would reinforce just how developed and mature as a Nation we are. It would constitute a more evolved and enlightened civilizational state, in as much as a changing of an age; a social and cultural historical step change in who we are as British people.

As far as my Christmas and New Year wishes go, this would be in my top three...

James Alistair Kirkcaldy, Wales/Cymru

The practice of peace and reconciliation is one of the most vital and artistic of all human actions.

—Thich Nhat Hanh (1926-2022), writer, teacher and peace activist.

Hope

Hope in the sunshine, as day awakes,
Hope in the sunset, as twilight takes,
Hope in the waking of a brand new morn,
Hope in the eyes of someone you adore.

Hope in loved ones, as they lay buried in peace,
Hope in the children running, playing, after the cease.
Hope in the world, as solidarity rises,
Hope in believing—united, we go marching.

Hope in humanity, as voices awake,
Hope in a future where love's embrace takes.

Shahd Karaeen, Palestine

Hope

Hope's not quite as it seems,
it's slimmer than you'd think
and less steady on its feet.

Sometimes, it's out of breath
can hardly see ahead
and cries itself to sleep.

It may not tell you all this
or the times it cheated death
but, if you knew it, you'd know
how Hope can keep a secret.

Yahia Lababidi, USA

What To Bring To A War Protest

Bring a candle
burning in your eyes
to lead the way,

bring a bird
nestled in your heart
to set others free

bring a shroud
large enough to bury
the dead past

bring a flag
spotless and white
to surrender pain.

Yahia Lababidi, USA

Alternative Scenario

After the horrors of October 7
the good people of Palestine rushed
to the sides of stricken Israelis

Tending to the wounded,
mourning the dead,
comforting survivors

They kept vigil, praying and weeping
delivering truckloads of flowers
serving trays, by day, of warm meals and sweets

Palestinian families flooded the streets
en masse, protesting: Not in our Names
demanding the return of hostages

Recognizing the great need, they gifted
what they, too, longed for: mercy, solace, solidarity—
and the world, witnessing, never forgot...

Helpless, Hamas eventually surrendered,
the Israeli government, in turn, relented
and walls in hearts crumbled, then tumbled.

Yahia Lababidi, USA

Our goal must be not peace in our time, but peace for all time.

—Harry S. Truman

Promoting Peacful Cultures In Local Communities

"It is through collective efforts and a commitment to peace that local communities can thrive and create a better future for generations to come."

Promoting a peace culture in local communities is a multifaceted endeavour that requires a comprehensive approach. The implementation of the measures would help communities to create an environment that fosters harmony, understanding, and cooperation among its members. This essay elaborates on each measure for promoting peace culture in local communities, namely conflict sensitivity, participation in peace endeavours, encouraging dialogue and mediation, promoting inclusion, supporting reconciliation and healing, addressing underlying grievances, and strengthening communication.

1. Conflict Sensitivity

Developing conflict sensitivity involves an understanding of the dynamics and causes of conflicts within a community. By promoting conflict sensitivity, communities can avoid exacerbating conflicts and instead work towards peaceful resolutions. Being sensitive to conflicts means community members can navigate their actions and policies in a way that minimises tension and promotes peaceful resolutions. Conflict sensitivity requires individuals to actively listen and empathise with the concerns and grievances of others, allowing for a more nuanced understanding of the underlying issues.

2. Participation in Peace Endeavours

Encouraging community members to actively participate in peace-building initiatives is essential. This can be done through organising workshops, forums, and events that provide opportunities for individuals to share their perspectives, engage in dialogue, and contribute to peace building efforts. Active participation fosters a sense of ownership and empowers community members to take responsibility for creating a peaceful environment.

3. Encouraging Dialogue and Mediation

Communities can promote dialogue by creating safe spaces for open and respectful communication. Mediation can also be employed to facilitate peaceful negotiations and find common ground among conflicting parties. Dialogue provides a platform for community members to express their concerns, fears, and aspirations in a safe and respectful environment. It allows conflicting parties to listen to each other's perspectives, find common ground, and work towards mutually beneficial solutions. Mediation, on the other hand, involves the intervention of a neutral third party who facilitates the negotiation process between conflicting parties. Mediators help to bridge the gap in communication, guide the parties towards peaceful resolutions, and ensure that all voices are heard and respected.

4. Promoting Inclusion

Inclusivity involves ensuring equal participation and representation of all community members, regardless of their background, gender, ethnicity, or social status. Through promoting inclusion, communities can address inequalities and foster a sense of belonging and shared responsibility. Embracing diversity and providing equal opportunities for all would enable communities to foster a sense of belonging and shared responsibility. Inclusive practices involve actively seeking input from marginalised groups, addressing power imbalances, and creating an environment where everyone feels valued and respected.

5. Supporting Reconciliation and Healing

Communities must support the process of reconciliation and healing for individuals and groups affected by conflicts. Reconciliation involves the restoration of relationships and trust between individuals and groups that have been divided by conflict. It requires acknowledging past injustices, providing space for truth-telling, and promoting forgiveness and understanding. Communities can support reconciliation by organising truth and reconciliation commissions, providing psychosocial support to individuals affected by conflict, and promoting initiatives that foster empathy and healing.

6. Addressing Underlying Grievances

In an effort to promote lasting peace, it is essential to address the underlying grievances that fuel conflicts. Conflicts often arise due to underlying grievances related to inequality, injustice, discrimination, and economic disparities. Through identifying and addressing these root causes, communities can create an environment that is less prone to conflicts. This may involve implementing policies that promote social and economic justice, ensuring equal access to resources and opportunities, and addressing systemic issues that perpetuate inequality.

7. Strengthening Communication

Communities can enhance communication by promoting transparency, providing access to information, and encouraging active listening. This can help prevent misunderstandings, resolve conflicts, and promote a culture of peace. Effective communication is the key to building trust, resolving conflicts, and fostering understanding among community members.

This may involve establishing communication channels that facilitate open and honest dialogue, promoting constructive feedback, and ensuring that diverse perspectives are valued and included in decision-making processes. Strong communication networks enable community members to express their concerns, share information, and collaborate effectively, thereby contributing to the overall peace building efforts.

Implementing these measures can contribute significantly to promoting a peace culture in local communities. It requires the active involvement and commitment of community members, leaders, and organizations. By implementing these measures, communities can create an environment that values peace, understanding, and cooperation, thereby fostering sustainable development and well-being for all its members. It is through collective efforts and a commitment to peace that local communities can thrive and create a better future for generations to come.

Dr. Muhammad Abdullahi, Nigeria

Peace: Humanity's Path To Hope

Peace is not merely the absence of war, but a profound state of harmony experienced by individuals, communities, and nations. It is a timeless dream that humanity has sought to achieve, serving as the cornerstone for survival and growth. In a world where conflicts and disputes are increasingly prevalent, the need to promote the values of peace and actively resolve conflicts has become more urgent than ever. But how can peace be practically and sustainably achieved? The answer lies in blending thought with action, dialogue with implementation, and faith in humanity with our collective commitment to peace.

Peace begins with individuals. Everyone has a role to play in creating an environment that fosters understanding, respect, and tolerance. Education is one of the fundamental pillars of promoting a culture of peace. When children learn from an early age the values of cooperation and understanding instead of competition and conflict, they become equipped to handle challenges and disagreements in peaceful and constructive ways. Schools are not just places to teach sciences and knowledge but can serve as centres to spread awareness about peace and implement its principles on both individual and community levels.

Diplomacy and dialogue also play a vital role in building peace on a national and international scale. Conflicts cannot be resolved through violence but by sitting at the negotiation table and listening to the other side. This is where international mediation and peace organizations come into play, tirelessly working to bridge gaps and propose solutions. Numerous examples of successful dialogue exist, such as peace agreements that have ended prolonged wars and restored hope to millions.

Peace is not only built with words but also through actions. Charitable work and community initiatives aimed at addressing the root causes of conflict, such as poverty, discrimination, and lack of opportunities, are critical in achieving peace. When people's basic needs are met, the likelihood of conflict decreases. Social and economic justice is a fundamental foundation for any sustainable peacebuilding.

It is essential to recognise that peace is not a permanent state; it is an ongoing process that requires collective effort. This underscores the importance of peaceful movements and activism that raise awareness and provide practical models for achieving peace. Peace activists play a crucial role in changing mindsets and inspiring communities to move toward a better future. Whether working in conflict zones or organising awareness campaigns, these individuals are the unsung heroes making a real difference in the world.

Peace is not an impossible dream but a choice we must all commit to. Through education, dialogue, and collective action, we can build a world of harmony and justice. The hope for peace begins in our hearts and is realized through our actions. Let us all be advocates and builders of peace, planting its seeds in every corner of this world. Peace is the true legacy we can leave for future generations.

Taghrid Bou Merhi, Lebanon/Brazil

A Laurel Will Blow Even More Freely (Freedom And Peace)

I knew this time would come
amorphous to the pore and no sensation
cross memory on a small screen
narcissism in the mirror of great loneliness
nothing social,
    nothing surreal
            nothing until tomorrow
why this world has spirits roaming around us
and feels then their oblivion
is a summary of wings that goes much further,
in the shed blood of those who believed they would be different
just a refraction of the new show.
Let's think more to go gray and more
on ridges bleached with the colours of the mountain peaks
covered with snow and wrinkled rocks from avalanches,
a little more, violet and rosemary when we start the harsh fires of our beard
a laurel will blow even more freely.

Agron Shele, Albania/Belgium

Peace, The Final Frontier

"You must cherish one another. You must work—we all must work—to make this world worthy of its children."

—Pablo Casals (1876 - 1973)

Sometimes it helps to rely on fiction to see a truth, or at least something, anything at all.

Suppose the Klingons and the Romulans (*Star Trek*) are involved in a bitter, terrible war. They each say the other side started it. The Romulans say the Klingons started the war eighty years ago. The Klingons say the Romulans started the war last month. That makes no sense until one understands that each side sees their shared past completely differently.

So, each side is oblivious of the other, and contemptuous to the other. When children of Klingons are taught geo-astronomy, they learn that both warring planets really belong to the Klingon world. The Romulans are usurpers in 'Klingonworld,' pure and simple. Klingon history says so.

When children of Romulus are taught geo-astronomy, they learn that the Klingon planet does not really exist at all, and never has. The Klingon history is a Big Lie. There is no Klingon history. The teachers concoct a different story about why Klingons exist, and where Klingons came from. In fact, the Romulan children are taught Klingons are not Klingons at all. They are just monsters.

The real problem with these two civilisations, though, is moral—as well as economic. How much is a life worth? The Klingons say that one of their own lives is worth one hundred Romulan lives. Only Klingons have names. Romulans don't.

The Romulans say the opposite, and then some—one Romulan life is worth one thousand Klingon lives. Only Romulans have names. Their deaths in the war are mourned with elaborate funerals and precious memories. Klingon deaths in the war are reported blandly and quickly as statistics. If the deaths are reported at all.

It is left to a Vulcan observer of this shared past—and this present war—to see the whole moral and economic problem which weighs mightily on the future of both of these two worlds. The Vulcan suggests to each side this thought. "You can start by understanding that the value of a life and value of the security of a Romulan child is perfectly equal to the value of a life and the value of the security of a Klingon child."

The Vulcan then raises one eyebrow, and says, with that characteristic dry irony that often expresses itself on their own planet as the closest thing to humour or emotion. "All children are innocent of crimes, especially war crimes. All children's lives matter. That is impeccable logic. From that realization, that step, you might advance a few steps toward peace, toward educating yourselves, to living differently in your future, and to finally prospering."

Don't you wish it was that simple on Earth? Maybe it is. Peace to all, goodwill to every Human.

Steve Huenneke, Ireland

Llavors De Concordia

En un món de crits illuites,
el mestre és el far serè,
en el mar de la discòrdia,
en la foscor del bosc.

Amb paciència i saviesa,
sembra llavors de concòrdia,
ensenyant a cada ànima
a ser lliure en la diversitat.

Cada lliçó és un pont,
que uneix les diferències
de les emocions rampants,
de les idees banals.

Amb paraules d'amor
ens parla de comprensió,
de la forca del diàleg,
dels cors sense rancor,

Amb la veu suau i clara,
ens recita apassionadament:

La Pau no és l'absència
de guerra o conflicte ardent,
és un estat de consciència
és l'amor que ens uneix.

Xavier Panades I Blas, Catalonia/Wales/Cymru

Seeds Of Harmony

In a world of cries and struggles,
the teacher is the tranquil beacon
in the sea of discord,
in the darkness of death.

With patience and wisdom,
sows seeds of harmony,
teaching each soul
to respect diversity.

Each lesson is a bridge
that unites the differences
of rampant emotions,
of trivial ideas.

With words of love
speaks of understanding,
of the strength of dialogue,
of hearts without rancour.

With a soft and clear voice,
fervently recites:

Peace is not the absence
of war or burning conflict,
it is a state of consciousness,
it is the love that binds us.

Xavier Panades I Blas, Catalonia/Wales/Cymru

Freedom and Peace

In a world where shadows of war loom,
Freedom cries out for a heaven without pain.
Peace, a distant dream, yearns to be real,
And the human heart, for tranquillity.

The violence of weapons destroys dreams, lives,
And sows hatred, where love should flourish.
But there is still hope, amidst the chaos,
For freedom and peace, are sacred rights.

May the leaders of the world, join hands,
To build bridges, and not walls of hate.
May education and love prevail over fear,
And peace be the refuge, where all find rest.

May freedom be a song,
That echoes endlessly, in every heart.
And may peace be the beacon,
That guides humanity, to a better future.

Adao Wons, Brazil

Wish

Let's turn swords into plows.
Iron can hurt the ground
or bring hope for a good harvest.

Let's convert the time of war,
full of hate and destruction,
to ages of abundance and happiness

Let there be only a gun
as a museum exhibit
in our new world of peace.

Alicja Maria Kuberska, Poland

And he shall judge among the nations, and shall rebuke many people, and they shall beat their swords into ploughshares, and their spears into pruning hooks: nation shall not lift up sword against nation, neither shall they learn war anymore.

—Isaiah 2:4

Biographies of Contributors

Dr. Muhammad Abdullahi is an academic at the University of Maiduguri, Nigeria, with numerous scholarly publications to his credit. He is actively engaged as a consultant and volunteer in peacebuilding and development initiatives. His peacebuilding work spans conflict mediation, facilitation of community dialogues, peacebuilding trainings, reconciliation of disputing groups, and the reintegration of victims of conflict across Nigeria. Beyond his professional engagements, he is deeply committed to mentoring and inspiring young people, leveraging his role as a university lecturer to promote community development and nurture resilient youths.

Derick Armah is a British Ghanaian poet, photographer and sound artist. His piece is themed around the potential of imagination and empathy as the precursors for all radical political action.

Gemma Barnett is an award-winning poet, writer and actor from London. She is a Genesis and JLF 2025 emerging writer/poet. Her published poetry can be found in *Propel Literary Magazine, Verve Poetry Press, Propel Anthology, Anthropocene Journal, The Passionfruit Review* and *The Pomegranate.* She was a winning finalist for BBC Words First 2022 and her poem 'My Abortion was Funny' was selected for the Verve Poetry Festival Anthology on Protest and commended in the Southbank Centre Outspoken Poetry Prize 2023. Her award-winning debut short film 'Bridge' was funded by the BBC after she was selected for the Talent Development Scheme.

Amber Berry is a poet from Bolton, UK. She started her poetry journey during the last lockdown, and has been attending poetry open mic nights over the past two years.

David Betteridge has been writing since his twenties, but without publishing until his sixties, when his *Five Glasgow Poems* was accepted by Raymond Ross for Cencrastus (2002). Since then, four books have followed (published by Smokestack Books and Culture Matters), the most recent being *Sapling & Wood* (2024), and *The Olive Branch* (2006), as well as a dozen poetry pamphlets, co-produced with the book designer, Tom Malone (Rhizome Press). Latterly, with Bob Starrett, Owen McGuigan and others, he has experimented with mixing verse with prose, images, and music, inspired in part by John Berger's work.

Xavier Padades I Blas (aka The Poetry Beast) is a Catalan writer and performer in Catalan, English and Castilian, currently based in Abertawe (Cymru). His bilingual poetry collections are *The Ear of Eternity* (*L'orella de l'eternitat*) (Francis Boutle, 2019) and *The Eye of Reality* (*L'ill de la realitat*) (Francis Boutle, 2023), and include themes of love, identity, and injustice. Xavier's tales and verses find a home in distinguished international publications such as *THE POET, Wales Haiku Journal, Presence, Azahar, Haus-a-rest Art Zine, Time Haiku, The Seventh Quarry*, and *Land of Change* (Culture Matters).

Heather Booker is a writer, trade unionist and socialist. She has worked in education and social services and the NHS and been member of Stop the War for years. She writes to avoid having to swear at the telly as politicians of all kinds vote for more war and arms while kids starve and wars' victims drown in the channel. She joined the Socialist Worker's Party in 1986 as nobody else seemed to be angry at austerity or doing anything about it; without justice there will be no peace.

Karen Gemma Brewer is a writer, singer and actor from Ceredigion. Born of coal-mining and farm-working stock, she combines emotion and mundanity with a strong sense of the absurd, is published in the UK, Europe and USA and translated into several languages. Her third poetry collection: *More Scarecrow Than Pirate* was published by Mosaïque Press in 2025, together with a volume of selected poems *Dandelion in the Sun*. A two-time winner of the Tim Williams Performance Poetry Award, Karen Gemma appears frequently on stage, radio and screen. Between tours she runs Gwisgo Bookworm book and record shop in Aberaeron with life partner Niki.

Cat Brogan is a poet from Omagh, Northern Ireland. She is the 2024 Ulster Poetry Slam Champion, a BBC Edinburgh Fringe Slam Champion, and represented Dublin at UNESCO Slamovision (2025). Her work has been published by Dedalus Press, *Skylight 47* and others. She holds an MA in Writer/Teacher from Goldsmiths, University of London, and is currently developing her debut poetry collection.

Kazimierz Burnat is a Polish poet, essayist, translator of Slavic literature, journalist and literary critic. He has authored 31 books of poetry, including eight in translation, and over 60 collective translation books. He is co-author of over 400 anthologies and monographs and is the organiser of the International Poetry Festival Poets Without Borders in Polanica-Zdrój. Awards include the Silver Medal For Merit to Culture Gloria Artis, the Minister of Culture and National Heritage Award for creative achievements (2023), and Shabdaguchha International Poetry Award for significant contribution to world poetry (USA/Bangladesh 2023). He is President of the Lower Silesian Branch of the Polish Writers' Union (ZLP) in Wrocław.

Scott Cassidy is an Edinburgh-based poet who explores the stories we tell ourselves to try and make sense of chaos. He has read widely, from the Edinburgh International Book Festival to the launch of an eco-collective's fight against climate change, and has been published regularly. He performs throughout the UK and sees poetry as a tool with which to fight back against those who choose profit over people and peace.

Guinevere Clark PhD (Creative Writing) is founder of Poetry Into Light CIC—empowering poetic voices, activating creativity and breaking down barriers in the literary world. Published widely in *Poetry Wales, Atlanta Review, Magma, Minerva Rising* and beyond, she won the 2024 Hammond House International Poetry Prize, was shortlisted for the Wales Poetry Award, Cinnamon Literature Prize and longlisted for the Nature Chronicles Prize. Guinevere writes on survivor narratives, nature, relationships, motherhood and sexuality, holds an MA in Creative Producing and coedits with Demeter Press. Her second collection, *Gift of Venus*, is due from Black Bough Poetry in 2026. www/poetryintolight.org

Derek Davies is a semi-retired builder, originally from the Swansea area. He moved to Port Talbot in South Wales in 1994. He started out on the road of poetry through his lifelong love of playing guitar and writing song lyrics; inspirational poets to date are Manchester's Tony Walsh and Wrexham spoken word poet Evrah Rose.

Tim Davies is a visual artist who has exhibited and made work over many years in Wales, the UK and internationally. He was selected for the inaugural Artes Mundi Visual Arts Prize exhibition in 2004 and was chosen to represent Wales in a solo show at the Venice Biennale of Art in 2011. His work interrogates contemporary sociopolitical and cultural contexts, using two and three-dimensional and performative media. His current practice explores the written, spoken and visualised word.

Binod Dawadi is a polymath from Kathmandu, Nepal, and a beacon of creativity, intellect, and activism. Armed with a master's degree in English, Dawadi wields the power of words to enact societal change. His journey as a writer, teacher, artist, photographer, model, and singer is a testament to his boundless passion.

Peter Devonald is a Forward Prize, Pushcart Prize and twice Best-Of-Net nominee. Winner Broken Spine Readers' Choice Award 2025, Loft Books Best Poem 2025, Heart of Heatons 2023 & 2021 and Waltham Forest. Extensively published including six Broken Spine anthologies, Broken Sleep, *Abridged, Alchemy Spoon, IS&T, Seventh Quarry, Full House, Shine* and *The Spectator*. Runner-up Shelley Memorial and N2tS. Finalist Tickled Pink, commended Poetry Café, Bermondsey & Beyond, Hippocrates and *Passionfruit Review*, Saveas & Allingham. 50+ film awards, former senior judge/ mentor, Peter Ustinov Awards (iemmys), Children's BAFTA nominated, Poet-in-Residence *Haus-a-Rest*, editor of *The Post* newspapers and *Poetry Corner*, and judge of Whispering Wisdom.

Dr. Kate Dewes ONZM (born 1953) is a New Zealand campaigner for disarmament and former advisor to two United Nations Secretaries-General. She was appointed an Officer of the New Zealand Order of Merit in the 2001 New Year Honours, for services to the peace movement. She successfully lobbied for the world's first national nuclear-free law, known as the New Zealand Nuclear Free Zone, Disarmament, and Arms Control Act 1987. She played a key role in the World Court Project that led to the 1996 historic judgement by the International Court of Justice, in The Hague, which unanimously ruled that a threat to use and the use of nuclear weapons is generally illegal according to international law. Along with her husband, former RN Commander Robert Green, she is co-founder and co-director of the Disarmament & Security Centre (DSC).

Manisha Dhesi explores belonging across nature, culture, and literature, inviting readers to discover their own voice in literature's expansive landscape. Deeply influenced by her Indian heritage, she explores the spiritual connection between nature, mental health, and societal norms. With a passion for representation and advocacy, she draws on her BS in Psychology and MA in Creative Writing to amplify diverse voices and create meaningful literary contributions.

Stephanie DuPont writes poetry to articulate what feels impossible to say, uncover new ideas, and explore the profound histories and small moments that shape our lives. She hopes her work offers readers a sense of connection. Her work has appeared in *West Ward Quarterly, California Quarterly, The Seventh Quarry, Snakeskin, Reach, The Dawntreader*, and *Highland Park Poetry*. A passionate advocate for nature, she has volunteered in the Florida Everglades and at Fairchild Tropical Botanic Garden.

Pam Evans MBE is the founder of the award-winning Peace Mala project for World Peace. She is an honours graduate of the University of Wales and is an experienced teacher of world faiths. Pam worked for over twenty years as the Head of Department of Religious Studies in a Carmarthenshire school in West Wales. Pam is committed to inter-faith dialogue for peace. She sees this as a vital process in the current world climate of fear and misunderstanding. Her creation of the Peace Mala was born out of the 9/11 disaster but was also influenced by personal experience and witness of intolerance and prejudice. In 2019, Pam received the MBE from Her Majesty Queen Elizabeth II for services to the promotion of peace and interfaith understanding. See www.peacemala.org.uk

Tim Evans (1949-2024) was a poet, activist, teacher, and co-founder of Live Poets Society, a radical socialist poetry group based in Swansea. His poetry has appeared in various anthologies, and in two previous collections, *Do You Want Some?* (2015) and *Exit 42* (2016). His artwork expresses his commitment to working with as many people as possible against racism and war.

Steve Gardiner is a professional musician and improviser, having studied at the universities of Oxford and Sussex. For over forty years he has been translating music into braille. He is an ordained member of the Sufi group Inayatiyya Healing UK, and a co-leader in the group's Prayers for World Healing vigils, which take place every month. He is a founder-member of The Peace Mantra Movement, and an experienced facilitator in meditation and sound healing.

Amy Garratt is a UK-based AuDHD Poet & spoken word performer, with an MA in Creative Writing from the Open University. Her poems have been published in various anthologies/magazines, and she indie-published two collections in 2021 & 2024. Her poetry includes AuDHD and mental health, alongside jovial and obscure musings. Her raw energy has drawn praise from the local spoken word scene, from performing at local festivals and hosting a spoken word night in her local bookshop from 2023-2025. She is currently an editor/judge at The Poetry Lighthouse @abg_writes_poetry (Instagram) ABG Writes Poetry (Facebook).

Barbara Anna Gaiardoni is an Italian pedagogist and author. Her Japanese-style poetry has been published in 285 magazines and translated into 12 languages. She is a winner of the 7th Basho International English Haiku Competition, a two-time Touchstone Award nominee (2023, 2024), and was recently selected among the European Top 100 most creative haiku authors in 2025. Her work has been featured in *The Mainichi*'s 'Best of' lists and received an Honorable Mention at the Fujisan Tanka Contest 2024 and 2025. Her poem 'Wounds Still Open—Ferite Ancora Aperte' is a World Gogyoshi poem according to the seven rules of the Taro Aizu.

Declan Geraghty is a working-class writer and poet from Dublin. He has had poetry published in *Shanghai Poetry Lab, Epoque Press, Militant Thistles, Cry of the Poor* and *The Brown Envelope Book.* His latest short story featured in *Lumpen London.* He has won a mentorship with Words Ireland, and is in their national mentoring program for new writers. He's recently won a scholarship place with *The Stinging Fly Play* It Forward programme, and been awarded a mentorship with *Skylight 47 Poetry.*

Johnny Giles is a radical tour guide, poet, journalism graduate and activist from Cardiff. His debut pamphlet *Chalk Outlines* was released by Blackheath Books in 2014. His tour *Poetry, Protest and Place* was developed in collaboration with Invisible Cities and Welsh homeless charity The Wallich in 2023. It was featured by various media outlets including BBC, Channel 4 and *The Big Issue.* He has survived call centres and homelessness, and is unsure which was worse.

Laura Grevel is originally from the USA and has lived in Europe for 25 years. She is a performance poet, fiction writer and blogger, tackling social justice, narratives and nature. Her work has been published widely, including in *Mayari Literature, Carnyx Collective Anthology Volume I, Poetry Salzburg Review, Masticadores Canada*, and *morphrog30*. She was shortlisted for the 2025 Bournemouth Writing Prize for Poetry and the Wolverhampton Lit Fest 2026 Poetry Competition.

Philip Gross is a long-haul traveller in the world of poetry, with nearly 30 collections, some prizes, and 30 years of work in schools and universities. Of 'Shore' he writes: 'You might be disappointed not to find this a campaigning poem, an activist poem, a propagandist piece for peace. That's not what I do (though I also respect writers who do). This one could be seen as 'about' a number of things—night, sea, the colour blue (it grew from a collaboration with an artist working in cyanotypes)... and sleeplessness, and letting go of life... and equally, yes, about peace.' 'Shore' is reproduced with thanks to *The Rialto* magazine, where it first appeared.

Richard Harries is a performance poet from Yorkshire. He has two books published by Stairwell Books of York: *Awakening* and *Iconic Tattoo*. A new book of poems about his abusive child/teen years and its effect on his mental health, called *The Black Dog Came To Stay* is published by Like A Blot From The Blue, Scotland. He writes with varied styles and genres, performing at festivals, community and charity events over the North of England and on Zoom events globally.

Dewi Heald is an author, musician and comic living and working in South Wales. His latest book, *The Great Stupidity*, a comic tale of education and AI, is currently available from Cambria Books. He has just released his second book of travels as a Quaker, *A Travelling Quaker Writes, Volume Two*—tales of visits to Quaker Meetings in the UK, Australia, Canada and Costa Rica.

Mererid Hopwood is a Professor of Welsh and Celtic Studies at Aberystwyth University, Fellow of the Learned Society of Wales, University of Wales Trinity Saint David and the Academi Gymreig, and Honorary President of the Waldo Williams Society. She is the secretary of the Academi Heddwch Cymru. She won the National Eisteddfod of Wales' Chair, Crown and Prose Medal and Welsh Book of the Year prize for poetry in 2016 for her collection of poems, *Nes Draw*. She has been children's poet laureate of Wales (Bardd Plant Cymru) and in 2018 won the Tir na n'Og prize for her writing for children. In 2023 she was awarded the Hay Festival Poetry Medal. She became the first woman in Eisteddfod history to be awarded the chair at the National Eisteddfod in 2001 which was held in Denbigh. In 2003, she won the Crown at the National Eisteddfod in Meifod, and in 2008, the Eisteddfod's Prose Medal for her book *O Ran*. In 2012, she was awarded the Glyndwr Award by MOMA, Machynlleth. She lives in Carmarthen with her husband and three children.

Steve Huenneke grew up in America, in Missouri. He was an economics professor for more than thirty years, and emigrated from America to Ireland. He is the author of *Farewell To America* (2025). 'Peace: The Final Frontier' is included in his latest poetry collection, *War Stories* (2026), published by Red Books Press, Wexford. Huenneke's poems contain thoughts, memories and feelings about both his life and about the condition and evolution of the world. He writes not under deadline, but as a lifeline.

Rhys Henry Hughes (born 1966, Cardiff, Wales) is a Welsh fantasy writer and essayist. Born in Cardiff, Hughes has written in a variety of forms, from short stories to novels. His long novel *Engelbrecht Again!* is a sequel to Maurice Richardson's 1950 cult classic *The Exploits of Engelbrecht* and is the most radical of Hughes's books, making extensive use of lipograms, typographical tricks, coded passages and other OuLiPo techniques. His main project consists of authoring a 1,000-story cycle of both tightly and loosely interconnected tales.

Gary Huskisson is a poet, a storyteller, a son, a brother and a father, once upon a time a social worker, a radio DJ, an athlete, a coach, and a wedding planner. Gary utilises art therapy as a way of making inroads into the cyclic nature of antisocial behaviour, making positive change for individuals and their communities. In his role of secretary of Peterborough Racial Equality Council and as a Spoken Word artist, he is now getting artists together from all over the globe to show the power of word in addressing racism in a project called SAY IT LOUDER, demonstrating the power of spoken word as a vehicle to change. His debut collection *Mile Stones* is available on Amazon.

Professor Uzo Iwobi CBE is a founder and Chief Executive of Race Council Cymru, Lead for Black History Wales, Coordinator for Black Lives Matter Wales Policy Collective, and a former Specialist Policy Adviser on Equalities to the Welsh Government. After qualifying as a barrister in Nigeria, Uzo moved to Wales where she founded Race Council Cymru. In 2004, she joined South Wales Police and in the same year, she founded the very first African Community Centre (ACC) in Wales and served as Chairperson for ACC for 15 yrs. Uzo served with the Commission for Racial Equality (CRE) UK as a Commissioner until it merged with the Equality and Human Rights Commission (EHRC) in October 2007. She is a fellow of the Learned Society of Wales, and a Fellow of the Royal Society of Arts. She recently co-founded the new Black Welsh Music Awards, the nation's first dedicated platform celebrating the transformational contributions of Black musicians to Wales' creative tapestry.

Mike Jenkins is a retired teacher from Merthyr Tudful in Cymru. Writes poetry in both English and Welsh. Former editor of 'Poetry Wales' and co-editor and founder of *Red Poets* magazine for 33 years. Organises poetry events in Caffi Soar, Merthyr. Winner of many prizes, including Eric Gregory Award, N. America Festival of Wales Welsh language poetry competition and Wales Book of the Year for a book of stories about young people from the Valleys *Wanting to Belong* (Seren). Has written several novels for young people and translated the ballads of Myrddin ap Dafydd for the book *Story of Wales.* Latest books: as editor *Yer Ower Voices* (Culture Matters), the first ever anthology of dialect poetry in English & Welsh from throughout Cymru; *Igh Sheriff o Merthyr* (Carreg Gwalch) poems in Merthyr dialect; *We Not Me / Ni Nid Fi* (Culture Matters) an anthology of radical poetry; and as author, *He Sings The Broken Cities* (Culture Matters).

Gareth Joseph is a Cardiff-based musician, poet and occasional writer. Recurring themes in his work include environmental issues and warfare. He says: 'The mountains of Wales are in my bones and the rain is in my blood'.

Hasan Kahya was born in Cyprus and is a poet and translator, living in London. After doing Business Studies, he worked in finance till his 'semi-retirement' which gave him the opportunity to explore the visual arts, psychoanalytic psychology, and poetry. His translation of the Turkish Cypriot poet Fikret Demirag was published in 2015 as a bilingual book, *In A Silence That Is God's Music*. Hasan's poems have appeared in various publications, including *The New European*. His poetry pamphlet, *The Pale Map*, was published by EWI in 2021.

Shahd Karaeen is a Palestinian poet, author, and Spoken Word artist. Her work explores survival, memory, womanhood, and resistance, weaving personal and collective histories through poetry and narrative. She is the founder of Peace Is the Song, a creative movement rooted in community, healing, and shared humanity. Through words, performance, and storytelling, Shahd creates space for voices often silenced, believing art can be both refuge and rebellion.

James Alistair Kirkcaldy is a full-time house dad. He trained as a sociologist and social psychologist, with specialisms in covert ethnographic research and other forms of social research, particularly in digital realms, and applied himself to antifascist and environmental activism. These days Jim can be found washing dishes, scrubbing toilet bowls, picking up other people's litter and growing food in his small permaculture food garden

Phil Knight is a poet and political activist from Neath, South Wales. He has supported CND, the Stop The War Movement and many campaigns for peace and justice. He has had poems published in *Red Poets, Atlantic Review, Roundyhouse, Poetry Wales, Earth Love, Planet* and many other publications. In 2014 Green Arrow published his poetry chapbook *Dylanation*. In 2015 the Red Poets published his poetry collection *You Are Welcome To Wales*.

Alicja Maria Kuberska was born in Świebodzin, Poland. She now lives with her family in the spa town of Inowrocław. In 2011 she published her first volume of poems, *The Glass Reality.* Her second volume, *Analysis of Feelings*, was published in 2012. The third collection *Moments* was published in English in 2014, both in Poland and in the USA. In 2014 she also published a novel *Virtual Roses* and another collection of poems *On the Border of Dream*. Her poems have been published in numerous anthologies and magazines in Poland, the USA, the UK, Canada, India and Australia. She was the featured poet of *New Mirage Journal* (USA) in the summer of 2011. Her poem 'Train' was nominated for the Pushcart Prize in 2011. In 2014 her poem was mentioned in the international competition *Nosside*. Alicja is a member of the Polish Writers Association in Warsaw. She is one of two editors of the artistic-literary quarterly journal *Metafora*, published by Miniatura, Kraków.

Yahia Lababidi, a writer of Palestinian background, is the author of 13 books of poetry/prose, including the critically acclaimed *Palestine Wail* (Daraja Press, 2024). Poetry from his *Wail* has been twice nominated for a Pushcart Prize and translated into Arabic, French, Malayalam, Gaeilge, Spanish as well as Dutch. Lababidi's poems for Palestine have also been read in literary festivals in the UK, Canada, Scotland, Holland, and at peaceful protests in the US as well as used in classrooms. His new book is *What Remains To Be Said* (Wild Goose Publications, 2025), new & selected aphorisms by Lababidi composed over the past three decades.

Alison Lochhead is an artist whose work reflects upon the fragmentation of memory and witness of injustices. Her work explores the impact war and conflict have on the world and on the environment: the destruction of livelihoods, identities, securities, homes, the migrations, the inhumanities, and the hope of change. Alison works with heat and materials from the earth, including iron, clay, rocks, oxides. Her peace-themed sculpture and artwork can be found atwww.alisonlochhead.co.uk

Jim Loft uses poetry as a way to explore both the amazing beauty of the universe, and also the deep pains of humankind. He runs the local U3A poetry group, an online international group, and belongs to the Swansea and District Writers' Circle. He lives in Swansea.

Mark Lyndon is a poet and singer based in Swansea, Wales, UK. He is a regular on the Welsh poetry open mic circuit, appearing at Talisman Spoken Word, Neath Poets, Yammer, and Swansea Fringe Festival. His publications include *Once More Unto the Beach, Dear Friends* and *A Bard's Eye View* and he has appeared in *Ten Swansea Writers* and Merrimac Mic's *The River Widens* anthologies.

Karen J. McDonnell's writing is widely published and anthologised, including *The Poetry Bus, Washing Windows V, Fire* (Arlen House), *Vital Signs* (Poetry Ireland), *Romance Options* (Dedalus Press), *New Isles Press 2, Skylight 47, Crannóg, The Stony Thursday, The Cormorant, The Galway Review, The North,* and *New Irish Writing.* Her poem 'Driftwood' was shortlisted for Irish Poem of the Year at the Irish Book Awards, while her non-fiction and poetry have been Best of the Net and Pushcart Prize nominated. Her collections *This Little World* and TIDAL are published by Doire Press. She lives in the west of Ireland.

Alan McGuire is a poet, writer, English teacher, and founder of *The Sobremesa Podcast*, and serves as an Associate Editor at Culture Matters. His work blends class politics, culture, and place-based storytelling across page, mic, and screen.

R.M. McKain is a detective noir novelist and a performance poet from the Welsh valleys known for his quirky outsider's view of the world. His debut poetry pamphlet *The Last Fly of Winter* is a reflection on masculine grief.

Ian J. McKenzie is a poet from Barrow in Furness, England. He has had his poetry published in several anthologies to date, including *Dissent: an anthology to end war and capitalism*, (Vagabond Books); and in *Ain't No Dead Beats Around Here* (*Like A Blot From The Blue*). He has also recently been nominated for the Pushcart Prize for Poetry for his poem, 'A Piet Mondrian View of Beach Life', included in *Ain't No Dead Beats Around Here.*

Simone Mansell Broome was born in Tenby and educated in England before returning to Wales in 2007. She jointly runs a venue for the arts, wellness, hospitality and eco-weddings on a small, organic farm. She writes poetry, prose and children's fiction, has been published widely in anthologies, ezines, magazines and websites, and has been on the radio. Three commissioned poems were filmed for ITV, and she has written special pieces for local groups. Her website is www.simonemansellbroome.com

Enzo Marra is a painter and poet based in London. He has been published in a solo chapbook *Prisoner of Observation* by the Shadow Archer Press, and included in the *Fool-saint AKA SOULFUL DISREGARDER*, a chapbook journal of new writing. In print he has been included in the *Sweet Dark Underbelly, White Chimney* magazine, *The Poetry Revolt*, and *Rattlesnake Review*. His poetry has also been distributed via bus display as part of BHAC Sussex Poetry Competition.

Taghrid Bou Merhi is a Lebanese-Brasilian multilingual poet, writer, author, essayist, editor journalist and translator. She has authored 23 books and translated 42 books and 112 articles to date. Her writings have been published several national and international magazines, newspapers, journals and anthologies. She was chosen among the 50 women from Asia who had a significant impact on the history of modern literature and she was chosen among the top 20 international journalists from Legacy Crown. She is a global advisor for poetry on CCTV Chinese TV and editor and head of the translation department at various literary newspapers and magazine and has been translated into 48 languages.

Mick Mezza has self-published *Worlds Apart* (poetry), *5 Shorties* (short plays) and *Lio's Road to Football* (children's book), and has performed poetry in Australia, Italy, England and Greece. He has had his poems translated into Italian, Greek and Chinese.

Dr Nela Milic is an artist and research professor with more than 25 years' experience of executing projects with artists, academics and community groups. Throughout her career, Nela has delivered creative projects for organisations including the Royal Opera House, Barbican, Arts Council England, John Lewis, Al Jazeera, Campbell Works, Oxo Tower, LIFT, and London Film Festival. Nela ran Refugees and the Arts Initiative—a British national organisation for the 'refugee arts'. Her work has been displayed at the Olympic stadium in London and she was part of the collaborative project by Vlatka Horvat at the Croatian pavilion of Venice Biennale 2024.

Davion Moore is an Ohio writer, who recently completed his Master's degree in Sports Journalism. He has written numerous poems and stories in the past few years. His poems can be found in works such as *Kapow!* (a superhero anthology), the Ohio Bards Poetry Anthology, *Things I Know Now*, and more. His stories can be found in Black Ink Fiction works such as *Truth or Dare, Winter Shocks, The Mummy* and *Infection.*

Dustin David Pickering's essay 'Knowledge and Mutuality' was presented as a speech to students in Nigeria in late 2024. Dustin Pickering is founder of Transcendent Zero Press. He is the author of numerous poetry collections and books including *Salt and Sorrow*. He placed in the top 100 for the erbacce prize in 2021 and 2023 and was a finalist in *Adelaide Literary Journal*'s first short fiction contest. He was given the honour of Knight of World Peace by the World Institute for Peace in 2022. He hosts the popular interview series World Inkers Network on YouTube and co-founded World Inkers Printing and Publishing.

Heather Pudner has lived in Wales for many years and has both Welsh children and Welsh grandchildren. She has written poems since she could write. After a career in Women's Aid, the civil service, education and widening access to higher education, she is now retired and fills her days with grandchildren, friends, re-homing junk, creative arts, folk music, writing and a bit of fun. All in addition to keeping a Left agenda alive in these difficult times.

Dr. Alok Kumar Ray is a bilingual poet who writes both in Odia and English. He has authored one English poetry anthology and one Odia poetry anthology and edited an international-level bilingual poetry anthology. He is a professor who teaches Political Science to students of different grades of study. He hails from Kendrapara district of Odisha, India.

Kevin Searle is a poet and street artist presently based in South London. His work employs a variety of forms to explore issues of race, class and identity in late capitalism. Searle's work has appeared in the anthologies, *Oluwale Now*, published by Peepal Tree Press in 2023, and *The Role of the Artist under Late Capitalism* published by Culture Matters in 2024.

Eliza Segiet graduated with a master's degree in philosophy at Jagiellonian University, Poland. She received a Global Literature Guardian Award from Motivational Strips. She was nominated for the Pushcart Prize in 2019, 2021, 2024. She received the Laureate Naji Naaman Literary Prize 2020, International Award Paragon of Hope (2020) and World Award 2020 Cesar Vallejo for Literary Excellence. Other awards she has received include: World Award Premiul Fănuș Neagu 2021, Bharat Ratna Rebindranath Tagore International Award (2022), World Poets Association Award (2023) and Laureate International Literary Award (2023).

Ian Sharp is a playwright. His play *Conchies* tells the story of a community of conscientious objectors (COs) that grew up around the villages of Legsby and Holton cum Beckering during the Second World War. Cast members included the ninety-nine-year-old sole surviving CO of the community, Donald Sutherland. The play was based on interviews with surviving members over many years, and tells the story of the community, its ideals and how the community broke up, mainly via their testimonies and with other scenes.

Peter Shaw is the Senior Publications Editor at Tearfund, a leading relief and development agency that works to end poverty and injustice, overseeing the production and distribution of *Tear Times*, a quarterly magazine that showcases the stories and impact of their work around the world. With a master's degree in playwriting from Goldsmiths, University of London, and a strong background in journalism, drama, social media, and digital media, he also collaborates with Tearfund's global network of partners, staff, and supporters to source and feature diverse and authentic voices and perspectives.

Agron Shele was born in Albania, and has written poetry books, novels and short stories. He has published 19 books, 13 anthologies and a serial in magazines and newspapers in Albanian and many other languages. He is President of the International Poetical Galaxy *Atunis* and co-ordinator of International Atunis Galaxy Anthology, and has won many international literary prizes.

Poonam Chawla Sood is a bilingual Indian author and translator whose literary work has been published across the globe. She is the founder and Chairperson of Gulzar Sahitya Samiti (established 1998) and an active member of various literary organizations. She has published six books, and received many national awards. She is also an awardee of Panorama International Golden Book Award 2024 for her book *TORN*. Her poems and short stories are regularly broadcast on All India Radio, Ayodhya. She has been an editorial board member of the Writers' International Edition 2024, and is currently an editorial member of *The Haril*—a Hindi magazine.

Richard W. Spisak Jr. began his work as a performer in Mel Tanner's Lumonics. Richard has written and produced a live sci-fi radio comedy series on WLRN-FM in Miami. He has seen six of his plays mounted, and has published two short story collections and three volumes of poetry. Richard also produces the webcast *Poets of the East* (interviews with international poets).

Bob Starrett worked in the building and shipbuilding industries, across Britain and abroad, and then became a mature student at the Glasgow School of Art. He then moved to working as a scene-painter in the film industry. He is the author of two books. *Rattling the Cage*- published by Ferret Press (1983), is a collection of his political cartoons. Most famous of his cartoons are those drawn for the UCS Work-in of 1971-72. *The Way I See It*, published by Fair Pley (2013), is a collection of memoirs, short stories, sketches, and cartoons, reflecting his experience both in shipbuilding and film making.

Antje Stehn is a German poet, visual artist, and art curator, who resides in Italy. She is a member of German PEN, co-editor of the poetry magazine *TamTamBumBum* and member of the directive committee of the Piccolo Museo della Poesia of Piacenza, Italy. Since 2020 she is curating the art-poetry project 'Rucksack: A Global Poetry Patchwork' and in 2023 'Hair in the Wind' which involved more than 250 international poets. She published the bilingual German-Italian books *Grotesk* (2022) and *Expeditionen and War* (2024).

Penny Stone is a community musician, activist and singer based in Edinburgh. She worked as a human rights observer in Palestine with EAPPI, the World Council of Churches' 'Ecumenical Accompaniment Programme in Palestine and Israel', and has been part of two solidarity choir tours to the West Bank. Penny leads radical singing in the streets and writes songs that help to uplift voices of oppressed people from around the world.

Martyn Sullivan is a writer and poet originally from Cardiff, now naturalised to Swansea where he works with spreadsheets. He is also a trade union steward. His short stories have been published in ergot, BFS: Horizons, Gwyllion and elsewhere, and his poetry has appeared in *The Seventh Quarry*. He is a member of Swansea and District Writers' Circle.

Richard Temple is a writer and poet from Wales, and published in the UK, India, Denmark, Japan, and the USA. His work draws upon the messy human experience, exploring aging, mental illness, politics and neurodiversity, challenging assumptions with authentic vulnerability through a lens of social alienation and absurdist humour. Richard performs regularly at festivals and events in the UK, and online. His multimedia work has featured in gallery exhibitions in Copenhagen and Lampeter, and he presented performance poetry workshops for Llandeilo Literary Festival. He's appeared at Morecambe Poetry Festival every year, from 2023-2025.

Sushant Thapa is a Nepalese poet from Biratnagar-13, Nepal who holds an M.A. in English literature from Jawaharlal Nehru University (JNU) New Delhi, India. He has published nine books of English poetry. These include: *The Poetic Burden and Other Poems* (Authorspress, New Delhi, 2020), *Abstraction and Other Poems* (Impspired, UK, 2021), *Minutes of Merit* (Haoajan, Kolkata, 2021), *Love's Cradle* (World Inkers Printing and Publishing, New York, USA and Senegal, Africa, 2023) and *Spontaneity: A New Name of Rhyme* (Ambar Publication House, New Delhi, 2023).

Lucilla Trapazzo is a Swiss poet, translator, artist and performer. A firm believer in human and planetary rights, her social and feminine perspective is reflected in many of her writings. To her credit she has nine books of poetry, a series of translations of international poets, numerous literary collaborations with associations, magazines and anthologies (as poet, editor, and translator), and a CD with compositions by Marco di Stefano. Her poems, translated into 18 languages, received important international awards including: poet laureate Kurora e Poezisë, International Festival of Korca, Albania 2023; first prize Civil and Philosophical Poems, XI Checkhov's Autumn International Festival, Crimea 2021; Golden Feather 2021 (Золотое Перо Руси), Russia, and she regularly participates in conferences as well as in international poetry, performance, and art festivals.

Gareth Twamley is a Cardiff-based poet and Spoken Word artist. He started his creative journey as an actor and quickly found his love for writing poetry. He has been actively combining both arts in the form of Spoken Word Performance since 2017. Gareth devised and hosted the Lyrical Miracles Open Mic and Word Asylum events in Cardiff and has recently experimented with the concept of 360 Immersive Spoken Word, using Full Dome Technology. Gareth has frequently written and performed activist poetry and is strongly opposed to fascism.

Pat Von Bismark is a British poet & writer from Sheffield, based in London. Through his work he creates visceral and rhythmic poems that match the increasingly dark and confusing world around us. This brief poem was written in the months after the Israeli invasion of Gaza and is written from the perspective of a small child.

Harvey Weedon is a British-Irish creative from Southampton, currently living in Manchester. A classically trained actor, his background is in theatre, both as a performer and a writer. Most recently his short play The Scene was staged at STOCKROOM for Not Long Stockport's inaugural theatre event. Alongside his acting career, he works with theatre charity Odd Arts, visiting schools and prisons around the north of England to deliver anti-radicalisation workshops using Augusto Boal's socialist Forum Theatre technique. He writes plays, screenplays, and poetry, exploring themes of queerness, Irish history, and student politics.

Adão Wons is a poet and writer, author of the book *Transparências —Evidências da vida e da alma.* He was the Honoured Author of the Cotiporã Book Fair in 2013 and Patron of the Cotiporã Book Fair 2017. Member of the IWA International Writers & Artists Association, Ohio, USA, Academician at the Accademia Internazionale Il Convivio in Italy, Universal Ambassador of Peace by the Cercle Universeldes Ambassadeurs de la Paz—Switzerland/France, Ambassador and poet of digital groups. Member of the Poetas Del Mundo movement Santiago / Chile. Member of the Hispanomundial Union of Writers. UHE Lima/ Peru. Member of the Venezuelan Society of International Art—Caracas / Venezuela. Effective member of the Partenon Literary Society—Porto Alegre-RS. Corresponding Member of the Academy of Letters of Teófilo Otoni—Minas Gerais. Corresponding member of the Cruz Altense Academy of Letters Cruz AltaRS. His poems have been translated into several languages around the world.

Rosy Wood-Bevan was born and brought up in the West Midlands, of Welsh heritage, and has been happily settled in her adopted hometown of Swansea for the past 20 years. She has written poetry sporadically for as long as she can remember, on themes reflecting her interest as a psychotherapist, on people, relationships, emotions and family history, as well as the natural world. She is a regular at Talisman in Swansea and People Speak Up in Llanelli and has had several published pieces in magazines and anthologies including *The Seventh Quarry* and *Red Poets.*

Notes on Images

Ch 1, Page 19. Artwork by Tim Evans

Ch 2, Page 39. Martin Luther King Jr during the 1963 March in Washington for Jobs and Freedom. Image: Rowland Schermann, US Information Agency. Source: Wikimedia CC.

Ch 3Page 51. India Gate, Kartavya Path, India Gate, New Delhi, Delhi, India. Photographer: Joshi Milstoner, Unsplash.

Ch 4, Page 63. Britain's Home Front, 1939-145 conscientious objectors attending a course in mechanised agriculture at an agricultural school in Essex, under the Ministry of Agriculture's labour training scheme. Source: Imperial War Museum, Wikimedia Creative Commons.

Ch 5, Page 81. Peace protests, images by Phil Knight.

Ch 6, Page 91. Coventry Cathedral (clockwise from top: the ruins of the old cathedral, reconciliation statue in the ruins, cross, interior stained glass window, interior and Cross of Nails. Source: Wikimedia CC.

Ch 7, Page 103. (Clockwise from top) Greenham Common gates, protestors at Greenham Common, peace campaigner Brian Haw, protest in London against the war in Iraq. Source: Wikimedia Creative Commons.

Page 104, A group of Welsh women show the Peace Petition from the women of Wales to the women of America. From left to right: M.G. (Gladys) Thomas; Mary Elizabeth Ellis; Annie Jane Hughes Griffiths; Elined Prys. (Harris & Ewing, photographer, public domain image Wikimedia Commons),

Ch 8. From top: Guernica mural in Lagunillas, Spain. Mural by Miguel Angel Chamorro. 2015. A mural reproduction of the painting by Pablo Picasso, *Guernica* (1937). Photo by Daniel Capilla (Wikimedia CC).Banksy mural in Bethlehem July 2015. Photographer: Za Banker, Wikimedia. Images CC. 'Food Not Bombs' mural, Berlin. Source: Creative Commons Wikimedia Images.

Page 119-120. 'Under (Found) Poems' by Kevin Searle, UK.

Page 121 (From top): The famous 'bed in' peace protest by John Lennon and Yoko Ono. Imagine Peace mural. Imagine Peace tower, on Viðey Island, near Reykjavík, Iceland. Source: Wikimedia CC images.

Page 127. Images from The View of Others from a Different Perspective, an art installation by Antje Stehn and Geneviève Seydoux, in Bern, Switzerland.

Page 129. The Red Dress Project. Image from Wikimedia CC.

Page 130. An image from the Novi Sad Protest. Image supplied by Dr Nela Milic. Ch9 Page 139 and 145, Artwork by Tim Evans

Page 162. Photo of Uzo Iwobi, Zero Racism Wales UK.

Ch 10, Page 183. Climate Change protest image and banner —Wikimedia

CC Ch 11, Page 197. 'Three Doves' artwork by Bob Starrett.

Page 203. 'Peace Gives Us A Chance'. Photographed by Steve Huenneke at SIPTU College, Custom House,Dublin, January 2024.

About the editor

Rebecca Lowe is a poet, editor and journalist, based in Swansea, Wales, UK. She is a Bread and Roses Spoken Word Award winner, and has appeared on BBC Radio 4 and Radio 3, and her poetry has featured in many anthologies, including *Red Poets, Blackheath Countercultural Review* and the *Ymlaen/Onward! anthology of radical Welsh Poetry* (Culture Matters, 2019). Her published work includes: *Blood and Water* (The Seventh Quarry, 2020), *Our Father Eclipse* (Culture Matters, 2021) and *Write Mindfully: Unlocking the Writer Within* (Talisman, 2025) and two shorter collections, *Ten Faces of the Virgin* (Talisman, 2025) and *The Road to Golgotha* (Talisman, 2026).

On *Our Father Eclipse* (publ. Culture Matters, 2021):

'A brilliant, inventive and original take on contemporary feelings of apocalypse, constructed around the image of a solar eclipse. Wide-ranging and eloquent, these poems barely contain their rage at the way we treat our neighbours and our planet in the 21st century. Black Lives Matter, Covid, global hunger, corporate greed, the refugee crisis and environmental catastrophe are all linked for Lowe by our collective inability to acknowledge our complicity in disaster.'

—Andy Croft, *The Morning Star*